THE
CELTIC
MISCELLANY

THE

CELTIC

MISCELLANY

BY ANDREW SMITH

VSP

Vision Sports Publishing
19–23 High Street,
Kingston upon Thames,
Surrey KT1 1LL

www.visionsp.co.uk

Published by Vision Sports Publishing 2009

Text © Andrew Smith
Illustrations © Bob Bond Sporting Caricatures

ISBN 13: 978-1-905326-71-6

Printed and bound in the UK by
MPG Books, Bodmin

Typeset by Palimpsest Book Production Limited,
Grangemouth, Stirlingshire

A CIP catalogue record for this book is
available from the British Library

Mixed Sources
Product group from well-managed
forests and other controlled sources
www.fsc.org Cert no. SA-COC-1565
© 1996 Forest Stewardship Council

FSC

Vision Sports Publishing are
proud that this book is made
from paper certified by the
Forest Stewardship Council

Foreword
by Billy McNeill

I don't know how to feel about the fact that, as chronicled in this book, it is more than a half century since I made my debut for Celtic. Old, I suppose, and it has never been easy coping with the advancing years.

Yet I could never have envisaged, when I made my debut in one of those old League Cup sectional matches in 1958, that I would enjoy a career of such success and excitement; so many of the great times and great memories recalled by all sorts of entries in the 150-odd pages contained here. I thank Andrew for being so kind to me in some choice statistics and curse him for forcing me to remember so many of them were clocked up so long ago.

I was a youngster when an injury to Bobby Evans gave me the opportunity to play my first senior match and still feel a youthful exuberance when coming along to Celtic Park for big games even now. The new stadium just creates a wonderful sense of occasion and how I would love to have played in so marvellous an arena.

When we ran out on to the pitch, The Jungle directly faced us and we got some incredible backing from a special place. But the deafening roar that can go right round the new stadium on European nights and Old Firm games must provide some gee-up for the players and I envy the current players when it comes to that aspect of playing for Celtic in the modern day.

Ultimately, though, I was so fortunate to have played for a wonderful club when I did because at a tender age I came under the influence of Jock Stein. He had just become the reserve coach when I came back from being farmed out with Blantyre Vics and there was a group of us he took in hand. Big Jock would give John Clark, Paddy Crerand, John Divers, Mike Jackson and me a lift to training in his car. He had such enthusiasm for the game and football knowledge and he saw those times in his motor as the opportunities to give us a real education in the game and impart his modern ideas. To have such a mentor at that time shaped my entire football life. And it is a privilege that Celtic was that life.

It was with immense pride that I managed the club and enjoyed some unforgettable times in charge but nothing beats playing the game. That is the essence of the sport. I know I have said in the past that I maybe retired early, in hanging up my boots at the age of 35 after I had captained the team to Scottish Cup success in the 1975 final against Airdrie. But, on reflection, I made the decision for the most positive reasons. I didn't stumble into the end of my career, which would not have been a pleasant way to bring a close to such a joyous decade-and-a-half.

Of course, then, if I have to pick the high watermark of my association with Celtic I can't look past the 1966/67 season and the European Cup triumph in Lisbon. I have to say, though, that while it might be described as an iconic image in this book, I wish the picture of me holding aloft the trophy didn't look as it did. It is a major regret that I was not allowed to pick up the trophy with all my team-mates around me because of a pitch invasion that was good natured and shouldn't have affected the presentation.

As we embarked on a season that culminated in us completing an unprecedented quadruple at the National Stadium in Portugal, we had no inkling such an achievement could be possible. At that time, filming began on a history of the club that meant a camera crew being given access behind the scenes to follow us through the whole campaign. I remember asking the director, Jimmy Gordon – the man behind Celtic Films, a group that would film games to show at supporters' functions – how he thought it would end up. "You just wait and see, everything is going to come right," he said.

That it did is so entirely in keeping with the rich history of the club. As I am quoted as saying in this book, I believe that things keep coming right for Celtic in a special way, one resulting in fairytales becoming reality, because the club was started up for the right reasons in a special way. There are many human stories told in this book of the special bond between Celtic and their supporters. I think these build a true picture of the cultural phenomenon the club has become.

The past is always the starting point when discussing what supplies Celtic with its greatness and, for me, why that will be without end. I'm just honoured to have played a part.

Billy McNeill

Acknowledgements

Apart from adding some fresh as paint new entries, the most pleasing aspect of doing the second edition of a book such as this is being able to, ahem, refine the odd oddity.

In that task I could have had no better assistance than was provided by Celtic historian Frank Glencross. Frank has been responsible for some important graft across a number of excellent books about the club, and too often his efforts seem to have gone unrecognised. I would like to give great thanks to a great man.

Otherwise, my acknowledgements remain as of first time around. Sincere gratitude goes to Jim Drewett of Vision Sports Publishing for the commission and his tremendous support. And cheers to Richard Bath for suggesting me as author.

Well, co-author, practically, with David McDonald's facts, figures and stats liberally drizzled throughout these pages. Another great man, I can't thank him enough. Same goes for Roddy Stewart. He offered similar help and a library of books. Cheers, also, to David Potter for filling in a few blanks.

My life would be all too blank without the love and blessings provided by my wife Sara and our daughter Sylvie. Sara's support, both materially and emotionally, throughout my daily wrestles with the written form is forever humbling.

Finally, thanks to my mum and dad for instilling in me a love of football and words. Thanks mum, for the football; thanks dad, for the words.

Andrew Smith

Author's note: All stats in *The Celtic Miscellany* are correct up to the start of the 2009/10 season.

— CHARITABLE BEGINNINGS —

Celtic's charitable foundations are now often blandly described as the club having been set up to help alleviate the crushing poverty that existed in Glasgow's East End during the late 1880s. However, to remove the Irish and Catholic from Celtic's origins is to deny what gave the club its impetus and identity.

Discrimination and deprivation ran hand in hand for Irish Catholics who had fled famine in their homeland to come to Glasgow in the 19th century. These factors fuelled the idea of a football club and account for why it was so powerfully and outstandingly realised.

Celtic's establishment came about through vision and chance. Brother Walfrid – born Andrew Kerins of County Sligo – a member of the Marist order and headmaster of the Sacred Heart School in Bridgeton, Glasgow, and formerly a teacher at nearby St Mary's, provided the vision. Determined to address the material and social disadvantages suffered by his community, he sought to tackle these through raising funds to maintain, what were effectively, soup kitchens.

The chance was Walfrid attending a reception at St Mary's Hall to celebrate Edinburgh Hibernian's 1887 Scottish Cup Final win over Dumbarton. Hibs were the foremost example of an Irish Catholic club in Scotland. Founded in 1875 by Father Edward Hannan, a priest in the city, players were required to be members of St Patrick's Catholic Young Men's Society, which was attached to St Patrick's church in the Cowgate area of the city's old town known as Little Ireland because of the concentration of immigrants.

At the cup-winning dinner, Hibs secretary John McFadden urged the people of Glasgow to found an equivalent club in the west of Scotland. Seeing first hand the popular appeal of the game, and the willingness of even the poorest to find the pennies to support it, Walfrid then made it his mission to do just that.

To this end, he unified prominent Catholic laymen – many active in Glasgow Irish political circles such as joiner and key facilitator John Glass – in a campaign to establish a senior football team in the only area of city that lacked one.

— MORE THAN JUST A FOOTBALL TEAM —

Celtic supporters like to claim their club, and their devotion to it, transcends football. Others will make that claim for them too:

"When you put on the Celtic jersey you're not just playing for a football team, you're playing for a people and a cause."
Former player and manager **Tommy Burns**

"There's an ingredient to this club that you can't quite put into words. I think it goes back to the very early days. I think it was founded for the right reasons and those reasons have stayed with us."
Former player and manager **Billy McNeill**

"The history of one of the world's great football clubs needs no embellishment from fiction."
Authors **Tom Campbell** and **Pat Woods** in the book *The Glory and the Dream: The History of Celtic 1887–1987*

"The best fans in the continent."
Spanish newspaper *El Mundo Deportivo*

"Celtic, like Barcelona, are more than a football club. Our clubs are a symbol of a culture and community that has not always been made welcome in their respective countries."
Barcelona player **Xavi Hernandez**

"A love affair we take with us to our death."
Former Celtic director and takeover rebel leader **Brian Dempsey**

"Our stadium is a phenomenal place, and it is difficult to put across just how much it means to play for this club, and what this club means to so many, and how well known it is in any part of the planet, until you experience playing at the stadium. Celtic is a way of life and very important for the Scots and the Irish, wherever they have emigrated to. And wherever you go, they applaud you and support you."
Celtic's Dutch striker **Jan Vennegoor of Hesselink**

"It's moments like this that you feel how deep-rooted Celtic is in society. Celtic is far more than a football club. The traditions, the history the warmth – you have to experience it every day to really understand this."
Vennegoor of Hesselink, again, on the 2007/08 championship win he dedicated to the late Tommy Burns

— MISSION STATEMENT —

As Celtic's official history has noted, ecumenism was hardly to the fore in the call to arms that formed the club's first major statement. Released in January 1888, it drew attention to Celtic's urgent need to raise funds among the community from which it rose:

'CELTIC FOOTBALL AND ATHLETIC CLUB, Celtic Park, Parkhead (Corner of Dalmarnock and Janefield Streets). Patrons His Grace the Archbishop of Glasgow and the Clergy of St Mary's, Sacred Heart and St Michael's Missions, and the principal Catholic laymen of the East End.

The above Club was formed in November 1887, by a number of Catholics of the East End of the City. The main object is to supply the East End conferences of the St Vincent de Paul Society with funds for the maintenance of the 'Dinner Tables' of our needy children in the Missions of St Mary's, Sacred Heart and St Michael's. Many cases of sheer poverty are left unaided through lack of means. It is therefore with this principal object that we have set afloat the 'Celtic' and we invite you as one of our ever-ready friends to assist in putting our new Park in proper working order for the coming football season.

We have already several of the leading Catholic football players of the West of Scotland on our membership list. They have most thoughtfully offered to assist in the good work. We are fully aware that the 'elite' of football players belong to this City and suburbs, and we know that from there we can select a team which will be able to do credit to the Catholics of the West of Scotland as the Hibernians have been doing in the East.

Again there is also the desire to have a large recreation ground where our Catholic young men will be able to enjoy the various sports which will build them up physically, and we feel sure we will have many supporters with us in this laudable object.'

— CELTIC LEGENDS: HENRIK LARSSON —

Henrik Larsson: Celtic's iconic No 7

There was much scoffing when Henrik Larsson was declared "world class" by Celtic general manager Jock Brown at the media gathering to confirm his arrival in July 1997. Brown's pronouncements were never knowingly modest but on this occasion he was spot on.

In seven years in Glasgow, the club's iconic No 7 proved himself easily the most complete player ever attracted to Scotland; arguably Celtic's most effective match-winner in the entire post-war era and, with 242 goals in 315 games, certainly the most prolific scorer the country has witnessed during that period. Although of wiry build,

Larsson was deceptively aggressive. He wedded ceaseless and selfless application to touch, awareness, invention and finishing prowess.

The son of Helsingborg factory worker Eva Larsson and Francisco Rocha, a sailor from Cape Verde, Larsson was initially treated with some suspicion by the Celtic support. His dreadlocks were his most outstanding feature claimed those who thought he had lost his way at Feyenoord. Celtic, reeling from contract difficulties with previous high-profile strikers, were considered foolish to touch the Swede, who himself had taken his previous employers to court over a £650,000 buy-out clause. During a now infamous debut, he passed straight to opponent Chic Charnley, who scored the winner for Hibs. But thereafter, Larsson did little wrong in Celtic colours. His imprint was on practically every Celtic success in the seven years that followed.

During his first season, Celtic ended a decade without a title by winning the 1997/98 championship. Larsson himself took centre stage with a sumptuous strike against St Johnstone on an emotion-drenched last day of the season. The high provided led him to remark, "I think we knocked on the head the idea that foreign players don't play for the jersey."

An insouciant figure off the field, his apparent aloofness merely added to his mythical status. As his goal-scoring became phenomenal, he achieved messianic significance for supporters. So much so that, by not playing, Larsson changed the entire course of Celtic's history. A leg break sustained against Lyon in October 1999 sidelined him for the rest of that season. But for this injury Celtic's management 'dream team' of Kenny Dalglish and John Barnes would probably have limped on, preventing the metamorphosis of the club that took place under Barnes's successor Martin O'Neill. This fusion of Larsson, the club's best player in 30 years, and O'Neill, the best manager in that period, underpinned a domination of the Scottish game Celtic hadn't known since the Lisbon Lions era.

The Swede also claimed Europe's Golden Shoe by netting an astonishing 53 times in 2000/01, including five of the six goals in the two cup final triumphs that delivered the club's first treble in 32 years. The following year Larsson again proved the single most significant figure in retaining the title and in his final campaign, 2003/04, he was once more Celtic's chief marksman as they claimed a third championship in four years.

The performance universally regarded as his crowning glory came in Seville. Yet two glorious headed goals from Larsson could not spare the club an agonising 3–2 extra-time defeat against Porto in the 2003 UEFA Cup final. However, his nine goals in earlier rounds had made possible the club's first European final in 33 years.

Typically, Larsson brought the curtain down on his league days at Celtic with game-winning interventions, weeping uncontrollably after two late goals secured a 2–1 win over Dundee United. The following weekend, he ended his Celtic career with a double that secured a 3–1 win over Dunfermline in the 2004 Scottish Cup final.

After leaving Glasgow, Larsson further enhanced his global reputation, engineering 2006 Champions League success at Barcelona as a super-sub. A "fun" loan spell with Manchester United followed. Hopeful rumours suggested a Celtic comeback in early 2007 but he signed another year with Helsingborgs. He did return to Celtic Park in May 2008, but only to play in a tribute game for former Celtic player Phil O'Donnell, who had tragically died of heart failure playing for Motherwell six months earlier.

Henrik Larsson factfile
Born: Helsingborg, Sweden, 20th September 1971
Appearances: 315
Goals: 242
Full international appearances while at Celtic: 49 caps for Sweden
Honours:
League championship: 1997/98, 2000/01, 2001/02, 2003/04
Scottish Cup: 2001, 2004
League Cup: 2000/01

— FINALLY, TWO DECADES ON —

The League Cup isn't supposed to matter any more. Yet, there was no way Celtic supporters were ever going to be blasé about their Co-operative Insurance Cup final success over Rangers on 16th March 2008.

The 2-0 extra-time win, earned with goals from Darren O'Dea and Aiden McGeady, was the club's first Old Firm final success in 20 years. That is the club's longest post-war period without cup-claiming success over their bitter rivals. Morever, it put an end to Rangers' three-final winning streak in such derby deciders.

— THE MEETING THAT MADE CELTIC —

Celtic Football and Athletic Club was formally constituted at a meeting in St Mary's Hall in East Rose Street (now Forbes Street) in Glasgow's Calton district on 6th November 1887.

While not all the founders were in favour, a key decision was taken to make the club open to all regardless of religion. This move was not supported by those who wanted the new body to be called Glasgow Hibernian to anchor it as an Irish club.

Arguing against this faction, Brother Walfrid strongly lobbied for the name Celtic (it was never Glasgow Celtic, as it is sometimes still wrongly labelled) – and won the day. This name was chosen specifically because it fused the Scots and Irish elements; both these races being Celts. The name was therefore Celtic with a hard C (K sound), not the soft C (S sound) it quickly became. Moreover, although Edinburgh Hibernian was the acknowledged model, Celtic was not to be linked to the temperance movements or the Young Men's Catholic society. Unlike the all-Catholic team in the east, Hibernian, religion was not to be a criterion when selecting players.

— UNFORGETTABLE GAMES:
START AS YOU MEAN TO GO ON —

Celtic 5 Rangers Swifts 2, friendly, first Celtic Park, 28th May 1888

There were a number of remarkable aspects to Celtic's first ever game. For one thing, it was astonishing that, only a matter of seven months after leasing six acres of disused land at the junction of Janefield Street and Dalmarnock Street (now Springfield Road) in Glasgow's East End, a ground had been created that boasted an open-air stand and pavilion, and had already hosted a friendly between Edinburgh Hibernians and Cowlair earlier that month. And it was an extraordinary coup that the first Celtic team featured James Kelly, the Renton centre half regarded as Scotland's leading international.

It was also fitting that Rangers, albeit second XI, should provide the opposition. That meant one of the bitterest rivalries in the world game can be traced to the moment Celtic was born as a football team, though relations between the pair were entirely cordial back then. And with the Irish Catholic club's opening encounter providing a competing attraction to a city visit by Queen Victoria, Celtic found themselves in opposition to the British Crown from the very off.

On an unseasonably cold evening – which, along with the royal visit, resulted in a smaller than expected 2,000 attendance – Celtic's opponents were effectively Rangers Swifts, the club's reserve side. The play of the fledging Celtic proved impressive, the 'ground team' clearly boosted by the presence alongside Kelly of fellow Renton man Neil McCallum. A few weeks earlier, the pair had played in the Scottish Cup holders' win over their English counterparts, West Bromich Albion, a victory that earned Renton the title of 'football champions of the world'. McCullum also had the distinction of scoring Celtic's first goal, a header. Kelly scored the second before Tom Maley bagged three, with Rangers' Suter making it 1–1 early on and then reducing the deficit to 3–2.

The Scottish Umpire said the new club's victory had been achieved "with a combination which could scarcely have been expected from an opening display". With great prescience, the writer added: "It would appear as if the newly-formed Glasgow club . . . has a bright future before it . . . If the committee can place the same eleven on the field as opposed Rangers . . . or an equally strong one, the Celtic will not lack for patronage or support."

Both teams were cheered off at the end and enjoyed supper at St Mary's Hall with the highlight of a convivial evening said to be Tom Maley's recitation of Victorian poem *The Lifeboat*.

Celtic: Dolan (Drumpelier), Pearson (Carfin Shamrock), McLaughlin (Govan Whitefield), W Maley (Cathcart), Kelly (Renton), Murray (Cambuslang Hibs), McCallum (Renton), T Maley (Cathcart), Madden (Dumbarton), Dunbar (Edinburgh Hibernians), Gorevin (Govan Whitefield)
Rangers Swifts: Nicol, McIntyre, Muir, McPherson, McFarlane, Meikle, Robb, McLaren, McKenzie, Suter, Wilson

— THOSE GLORY EARLY YEARS . . .
AT HIBERNIAN'S EXPENSE —

Celtic revitalised Scottish football with their formation in 1888 and were responsible for the sport's first attendance boom. The club represented a passionate and enthusiastic Irish Catholic community, giving them a focus to celebrate a culture so often treated with disdain elsewhere. This support was a potent factor in Celtic's early success. Equally important was the club's ruthlessly professional outlook, which played fast and loose with the conventions of amateurism under which the sport then operated.

Celtic's first victims were the very club that had been the touchpaper to spark them into life. Although there had been an understanding that they would not take each other's players, Hibs lost half a team to Celtic as the Glasgow side embarked on their first season in 1888/89.

The Edinburgh club's bitterness, understandably, did not subside for many years after 1887 cup winners Jimmy McLaren and Willie Groves, as well as Michael Dunbar, Paddy Gallagher, John Coleman and Mick McKeown, were enticed westwards through approaches and financial inducements that were highly illegal, but not the preserve solely of the new club. Celtic already had Scotland's best player in James Kelly, attracted from Renton, as a declaration of intent. They meant business. During a time when clubs frequently appeared then disappeared – Rangers, formed in 1874, struggled in their early years to avoid that fate – Celtic were determined to show they were here to stay. And the club soon proved it would be a major force in Scottish football with these early successes:

- In their debut season, Celtic reached the Scottish Cup final before losing 2–1 to Third Lanark and raised the huge sum of £330 for identifiable Catholic charities.
- In 1892, Celtic won the Scottish Cup for the first time with a 5–1 win over Queens Park and moved into a new stadium that representatives of the Football League in England declared "superior to any in Great Britain"
- In 1892/93, Celtic claimed their first title, two years after being founder members of Scottish League and finishing third in the inaugural championship of 1890/91. From 1891, until 1895/96

they dominated the Scottish scene with three titles, one Scottish Cup, four Glasgow Cups and five Glasgow Charity Cups.
• In 1895/96, Celtic's turnover was £10,142, then the highest ever recorded by any British club.

— SECOND TO NONE SERVICE —

With an incredible 790 games for the club, 'Lisbon Lion' Billy McNeill is Celtic's record appearance maker.

The top ten is dominated by post-war Celts, an inevitable result of the club's early players not having had the opportunity to play in Europe and the League Cup. The all-time league appearances list, though, is a mix of players from across the club's history.

Top ten all-time appearances (all competitions)

		Total
1.	Billy McNeill (1957–75)	790
2.	Paul McStay (1981–97)	677
3.	Roy Aitken (1972–90)	672
4.	Danny McGrain (1967–87)	663
5.	Pat Bonner (1978–94)	641
6.	Alec McNair (1904–25)	604
7.	Bobby Lennox (1961–80)	589
8.	Bobby Evans (1944–60)	535
9=.	Jimmy Johnstone (1961–75)	515
9=.	Jimmy McMenemy (1902–20)	515

Top ten all-time league appearances

1.	Alec McNair (1904–25)	548
2.	Paul McStay (1981–97)	515
3.	Billy McNeill (1957–75)	486
4=.	Roy Aitken (1972–90)	483
4=.	Pat Bonner (1978–94)	483
6.	Jimmy McMenemy (1902–20)	456
7.	Danny McGrain (1967–87)	441
8.	Patsy Gallacher (1911–26)	432
9.	Charlie Shaw (1913–25)	420
10.	Jimmy McStay (1920–34)	409

— MOWBRAY MAKES SENSE —

It seemed the most natural fit when Tony Mowbray was appointed Celtic manager in the summer of 2009. Even when he became the first former player to be handed the role in 15 years. Even when his recruitment made him the first English-born holder of the position. Even when, immediately before stepping in to a role from which Gordon Strachan had stepped down, he had suffered relegation from the English Premier League with West Bromwich Albion.

Mowbray's professional appeal is that, in his first job at Hibernian and then with Albion, for five seasons he made it, to a fault at times, his mission to play football the so-called 'Celtic way'. The emphasis was puritanically on free-flowing attack. Mowbray's personal appeal, meanwhile is that he is a man of great humanity. He elicits tremendous warmth from the Celtic support for the dignity he showed in dealing with personal tragedy at the club, which spanned four years from 1991. On New Year's Day 1995 he lost Bernadette, the woman he had met and married in his time in Scotland, to breast cancer.

That experience, and his creation of the pre-match 'huddle' (see 'Tony's Huddle' page 89) as a means of showing the players' togetherness, is what gives his Celtic story great resonance. It fuels the idea he is fulfilling a destiny in returning to a club that likes to celebrate strength of character in adversity and a certain romanticism.

— THE IN-A-ROW LIST —

Celtic's title success in 2007/08 put Gordon Strachan in the company of Willie Maley and Jock Stein as only the third manager to guide the club to three consecutive championships. Strachan, in failing to add a fourth consecutive league crown, has to defer to Maley and Stein:

Nine-in-a-row: Jock Stein (1965/66 to 1973/74)
Six-in-a-row: Willie Maley (1905/06 to 1909/10)
Four-in-a-row: Willie Maley (1913/14 to 1916/17)
Three-in-a-row: Gordon Strachan (2005/06 to 2007/08)
Two-in-a-row: Billy McNeill (1980/81 and 1981/82); Martin O'Neill (2000/01 and 20001/02)

— ICING ON THE EUROPEAN CUP WIN —

As Tommy Gemmell was weaving his way through frolicking fans on leaving the field at Lisbon after the club's 1967 European Cup triumph on 25th May 1967, he spied an ice-cream stall.

The scorer in the final believed his efforts might have merited a freebie. But on failing to provide any cash before walking off with his ice, Gemmell was cornered by the cone man until he found a journalist to stand him the scoop.

— SPL ALL-TIME TABLE 1998/99 - 2008/09 —

Celtic have dominated the Scottish Premier League in its first decade of existence, as this table clearly shows:

	P	W	D	L	F	A	Pts
Celtic	414	304	61	49	968	336	973
Rangers	414	282	76	56	876	333	922
Hearts	414	172	103	139	560	487	619
Aberdeen	414	147	98	169	499	587	539
Kilmarnock	414	146	100	168	507	591	538
Hibernian	378	137	97	144	526	526	508
Motherwell	414	133	94	187	500	630	493
Dundee United	414	112	115	187	451	636	451
Dunfermline	302	78	79	145	295	483	313
Dundee	262	80	61	121	308	412	301
Inverness CT	190	60	48	82	222	253	228
Livingston	190	48	45	97	205	306	189
Falkirk	152	45	35	72	166	212	170
St Johnstone	148	39	43	66	139	200	160
St Mirren	152	35	39	78	122	229	144
Partick Thistle	76	14	19	43	76	125	61
Hamilton	38	12	5	21	30	53	41
Gretna	38	5	8	25	32	83	23

— STRACHAN THE SUCCESSFUL DIVIDER —

When he addressed the crowd on the Celtic Park pitch at the Tommy Burns tribute game on 31st May 2009, Gordon Strachan spoke with warmth and humility, and in moving terms about the feelings he had developed for the club. Pity he waited until a week after he had resigned as Celtic manager to show there was much more to him than the chippy, defensive, wearyingly divisive figure he so often was in public forums during his four years at the helm.

Strachan's tenure was unarguably successful. Hugely so. Three title wins in four years and two Champions League 16s will forever be the riposte to the many who were far from sold on his stewardship of the club. But his time in charge certainly wasn't as satisfying for the Celtic support as the silverware triumphs – six in total – suggest it ought to have been.

Essentially, that can be attributed to the fact his record is much better than the football that fashioned it. He would argue that was outwith his control. The club could no longer afford players of the calibre attracted at the start of predecessor Martin O'Neill's time, and appeared to become fixated with a zero debt position.

Yet, throughout Strachan's era, Celtic operated with the highest wage bill in the country, and in recent years have extended their massive financial advantages over most Scottish Premier League rivals. If doing his job properly, translating such advantages into championship victories with a degree of conviction was the least entitled to be expected of him.

Much more was certainly expected than what he drew from his squad in his last months, a truly risible run-in that wrecked the 2008/09 season. Hopes of a fourth straight title evaporated in the sorriest manner imaginable. A seven-point lead was squandered as Strachan's side won only nine of their final 22 league games. Team and manager seemed to lose the will. It made for grim viewing.

The spiky little redhead tired, and supporters tired of him, in part because he constantly seemed at odds with the entire Scottish football world. A sufferer of the Napoleon complex, undoubtedly, lazy media reasoning had it that he was never accepted by the club's faithful because he wasn't a 'Celtic man' – not a Catholic, former player, supporter or Irish, essentially. That hardly explains why Wim Jansen is none of these but revered for one momentous league win. Strachan's personality became a roadblock to enjoying a smooth run at the club.

Four seasons can be divided into a two parts. Strachan, who had spells in charge at Coventry City and Southampton, ended a sabbatical from the game to take over from the beloved Martin

O'Neill in June 2005. He showed great fortituded to recover from that catastrophic 5-0 loss away to Artmedia Bratislava in the Champions League qualifier, and a 4-4 draw at Motherwell four days later. By the end of his first season, indeed, there were few Strachan detractors. For the man who enjoyed sticking it to Celtic as an Aberdeen player in the 1980s there was instead new-found respect. Gained after he reduced the club's wage bill and forged an entertaining new, young team in which his brilliant signings Artur Boruc and Shunsuke Nakamura were central.

His buys thereafter were decidedly mixed, but the team's form remained good as the title was retained the following season – and the Champions League group stages thrillingly negotiated for the first time. That feat in continental competition was repeated in his third season, but by now cracks were beginning to appear on the domestic front. Renewed by Walter Smith and sizeable spending, Rangers were transformed from the puniest of pushovers to a match for Strachan's team. The Celtic manager didn't seem able to derive the best from playing resources generally regarded to be superior to those at Ibrox.

In his third season of 2007/08, Strachan may have become the first man since Stein to lead the club to three consecutive championships. Yet, that had as much to do with Rangers wilting under a strain of a fixture pile-up caused by their participation in the UEFA Cup final as Celtic racking up full points from their final seven games to retrieve a seemingly impossible situation. Memories of that emotional success, made so by the death of Tommy Burns the previous week, will ensure Strachan is recalled with greater fondness than he generated when in the employ of the club.

— PARKHEAD IS A PLACE, NOT A FOOTBALL GROUND —

One of the many foibles of Fergus McCann during his five-year ownership of Celtic from 1994 accounted for the disappearance of the term 'Parkhead' in any club publications, even if Parkhead was the ground where, in the eyes of the club's supporters, their team played. Officially, Celtic play at Celtic Park in the Parkhead area of Glasgow and McCann demanded that the official terminology was always adhered to whenever the stadium was referred to in print.

— HOME GAME AT OLD TRAFFORD —

During their 1984/85 European Cup Winners' Cup campaign Celtic were forced to replay their second round home leg against Rapid Vienna at Old Trafford, after the original tie at Celtic Park was declared void by UEFA following crowd trouble.

Trailing 3–1 from the first leg in Vienna, Celtic appeared to have overturned the deficit with a 3–0 home win on 24th October 1984 against thuggish opponents who had Reinhard Kienast sent off for punching Tommy Burns on the back of the head. The Austrians, though, appealed against the result, pointing to an incident when a bottle was thrown from the Jungle. Although the missile clearly missed its target, Rapid player Rudi Weinhofer pretended it had hit him and left Celtic Park with his head swathed in bandages.

Initially, UEFA rejected Rapid's appeal and fined the Austrians' £5,000 for their unsporting behaviour. Then, UEFA accepted that Weinhofer had been struck – although by a coin, rather than a bottle – although, bizarrely, they also increased his club's fine to £10,000. More importantly, Celtic were ordered to replay the second leg at a neutral venue.

At Old Trafford on 7th November an ugliness hung in the air for a game that had no right to take place. A vengeful Celtic support of around 40,000 demanded that their team kill off the bogeymen from Vienna. The hostile atmosphere should have worked in Celtic's favour, but under intolerable pressure to win the players failed to develop a coherent strategy. Drawing strength from their unease, Rapid picked them off with a cheap 17th-minute goal, only seconds after Roy Aitken had hit the bar, to win 4–1 on aggregate. Nor was that the end of the nightmare. During the match a couple of supporters invaded the field and attempted to attack Austrian players. UEFA took a dim view of the incident and Celtic were forced to play the first game of their next European campaign, against Atlético Madrid, behind closed doors. They lost that too.

— YOU'VE BEEN HOOPED —

Celtic supporter Liam Graham of Alexandria in Dumbartonshire has recordings of every one of the club's games screened on television since 1979. Until the advent of DVD, his living room resembled an editing suite, with a wall of video tapes piled to ceiling height.

— ALTERNATIVE CAREERS —

A number of Celtic players could have pursued other careers full time if they hadn't concentrated on football. Among them:

Jim Craig: Qualified as a dentist while at Celtic in the 1960s. He practised after retiring, having kept his hand in working in Glasgow Corporation clinics while playing.
Harald Brattbakk: Qualified accountant.
Gordon Marshall: Continued to work in his father's hairdressing salon in Edinburgh while at Celtic, where he was hairdresser to the squad.
Allen McKnight: Worked as a navvy on the construction of the M25.
Ian Young: Apprentice industrial chemist.
Jimmy McMenemy: Chairmaker.
Charlie Shaw: Barker at Parkhead Cross fair.
Graham Barclay: Professional guitarist.
Jim and Frank Brogan: Bath qualified as chartered accountants.

— CHARITY ENDS —

Celtic may have been raking in money throughout their early years, but ever less of it seemed to find its way to the good causes the club had been founded to support. From the mid-1890s, officials claimed stadium and running costs and the advent of on-field professionalism demanded the raising of capital through Celtic becoming a limited liability.

On 4th March 1897, in the same St Mary's Hall where the club had been formed for charity, these noble ideals were sold out as agreement was reached on the creation of Celtic Football and Athletic Company Limited. At the first meeting of the new company on 17th June that year, John H McLaughlin was elected chairman to a board comprised of James Kelly, James Grant, John Glass, Michael Dunbar, John McKillop and John O'Hara. In the following year, another new British record for football income was set with profits of £16,267. Dividends amounting to 20 per cent of that were paid to directors and shareholders. Nothing was earmarked for charity. Brother Walfrid's Celtic had passed into history.

— CELTIC FOLK SAY THE FUNNIEST THINGS —

"There they were: Facchetti, Domenghini, Mazzola, Cappellini; all six-footers wi' Ambre Solaire suntans, Colgate smiles and sleek-backed hair. Each and every wan o' them looked like yon film star Cesar Romero. They even smelt beautiful. And there's us lot – midgets. Ah've got nae teeth, Bobby Lennox hasnae any, and old Ronnie Simpson's got the full monty, nae teeth top an' bottom. The Italians are staring doon at us an' we're grinn' back up at 'em wi' our great gumsy grins. We must have looked like something oot o' the circus."
Jimmy Johnstone describing the scene in the Lisbon tunnel before Celtic's 1967 European Cup Final win over Internazionale

"When they scored their third I actually thought they'd gone off to the town to celebrate."
Martin O'Neill on Porto's ridiculously over-the-top time-wasting goal celebrations in the 2003 UEFA Cup final

"See if you're inside the 18-yard box and you've nobody to stick it to – just stick it in the net."
Celtic coach **Jimmy Hogan**'s simple instruction to players in 1948

"A striker that can't score is like a joiner that can't saw."
Former Celtic striker and now joiner **Frank McGarvey** shows little sympathy for the plight of forward Kenny Miller during his 15-game barren run for Celtic in season 2006/07

"I think a lot of people turned up to see what people from Albania looked like."
Murdo MacLeod on 51,000 turning up to watch Celtic play Partizan Tirana in a first round European Cup tie in September 1979

"When I was at Celtic I was said to be a players' man and maybe that is true. In those days, if the ship was sinking, I would have thrown eleven lifebelts to all the players. Now I would keep one for myself, throw ten and lose a player."
David Hay, speaking in 1991, on suggestions he was too soft in his time as Celtic manager from 1983 to 1987

"He's not a bad lad, is he? If it said 'God bless Myra Hindley' I might have a problem with it."
Gordon Strachan, on being asked if he felt it was provocative that

his Polish goalkeeper Artur Boruc had revealed a T-shirt with a picture of Polish Pope John Paul II and the inscription 'God Bless the Pope' after his Celtic side's win over Rangers in April 2008

— CELTIC DOES DALLAS . . . AND VICE VERSA? —

Home defeats to Rangers always stick in the craw of Celtic's fans, but the 3–0 drubbing on 2nd May 1999 was especially unpalatable as it allowed Rangers to clinch the title at Celtic Park for the first time in their history.

Celtic let themselves down on and off the park, four supporters blurring that distinction by invading the pitch in an attempt to confront referee Hugh Dallas. The home crowd was incensed when Dallas sent off Stephane Mahe in bizarre circumstances after half an hour, the Frenchman twice having been booked for complaining about fouls against him. Dallas was later struck by a coin that caused blood to pour from his head, an incident which provided gruesome images in the following day's newspapers. Soon after recovering, he awarded Rangers a penalty for an infringement lost on everyone else. Jörg Albertz converted to put Rangers two up, and the game was up for Celtic. The visitors' Rod Wallace and Celtic substitute Vidar Riseth were both sent off in the final minutes.

— RED AND THE BLUE —

Alan Thompson is the only player to have been red-carded three times in Old Firm games:

Date	Result	Offence
26th Nov 2000	Rangers 5 Celtic 1	Second yellow for a rash tackle
20th Nov 2004	Rangers 2 Celtic 0	Straight red for a headbutt
20th Aug 2005	Rangers 3 Celtic 1	Straight red for a lunging tackle

— CELTIC LEGENDS: JIMMY QUINN —

Jimmy Quinn: the shoulders of a charging bison

Some Celtic historians choose to celebrate Jimmy Quinn as the club's first scoring machine; others as the only man to have netted hat-tricks in more than one Old Firm game of note.

Universally, he is recalled as a rampaging forward who would fearlessly fling his 5ft 8in frame through the air, and through opponents, in his goal-getting charges. Injuries, both suffered and inflicted, were a feature of a career during which he was acknowledged as a force of nature. Or as *The Celtic Story of 1960* wonderfully put it: "With the deep chest and muscular shoulders of a charging bison he shed festoons of clinging opponents as he hurtled goalwards."

Quinn, spelled 'Quin' on his birth certificate, had to be cajoled by Celtic manager Willie Maley to sign for the club in 1901. The modest Croy man, then playing for Smithston Albion in Stenhousemuir, felt that the juniors was his level and the pit where he belonged. Celtic directors wondered if Maley might have been better leaving him there when he struggled to settle on the left wing.

But the final of the 1902 Exhibition Trophy provided the platform for Quinn to demonstrate he had the character and courage to cause carnage when played through the middle. And his hat-trick in a 3–2 extra time win over Rangers led to Celtic being crowned unofficial British champions, with the tournament bringing together league winners and runners-up from both sides of the border.

Two years later Quinn repeated the feat in the 1904 Scottish Cup Final win over the club's great rivals. All three of his goals came after Celtic had found themselves 2–0 down at half-time. The triple frames his greatness for a club he helped to dominate the Scottish game. In the New Year derby of 1912 he scored a third hat-trick.

A player whose robust style led him to fall foul of authorities, Quinn was also sent off twice against the Ibrox club and accused of an intolerable wrecklessness in his approach. It led his protective manager Maley to offer in defence, "All the men that Quinn killed are still alive."

Celtic were outraged at the suspension that followed his second ordering off, an unjustified dismissal, and a fund was set up for him. It attracted donations from as far as New York and amassed almost £300. Quinn was too shy to speak at the concert to hand him it over, yet undoubtedly was one of the early football celebrities. He endorsed products, including Boag's Rheumatic Rum, but after seeing his face plastered on billboards to advertise a newspaper column, immediately wanted to end the lucrative arrangement.

Before knee injuries forced his retirement in 1915, Quinn earned 11 full caps and scored seven times for his country. Even almost a century on, his strike rate places him among the elite of the club's goal-plunderers.

Jimmy Quinn factfile
Born: Croy, 8th July 1878
Died: Croy, 20th November 1945
Appearances: 331
Goals: 217
Full international appearances while at Celtic: 11 caps for Scotland
Honours:
League championship: 1904/05, 1905/06, 1906/07, 1907/08, 1908/09, 1909/10
Scottish Cup: 1904, 1907, 1908, 1911, 1912

— NINE-IN-A-ROW —

Celtic famously won the league title for a record nine consecutive seasons under manager Jock Stein between 1966 and 1974. Here's how the top of the table looked in each of those campaigns (with points in brackets):

Season	1st	2nd	3rd
1965/66	Celtic (57)	Rangers (55)	Kilmarnock (45)
1966/67	Celtic (58)	Rangers (55)	Clyde (46)
1967/68	Celtic (63)	Rangers (61)	Hibs (45)
1968/69	Celtic (54)	Rangers (49)	Dunfermline (45)
1969/70	Celtic (57)	Rangers (45)	Hibs (44)
1970/71	Celtic (56)	Aberdeen (54)	St Johnstone (44)
1971/72	Celtic (60)	Aberdeen (50)	Rangers (44)
1972/73	Celtic (57)	Rangers (56)	Hibs (45)
1973/74	Celtic (53)	Hibs (49)	Rangers (48)

— HAMPDEN HOT AND COLD SHOTS —

In Celtic's treble-winning season of 2000/01, Henrik Larsson scored nine goals at Hampden, netting in both cup semi-finals and the finals played at the national stadium. In the 1994/95 season wherein Celtic rented Hampden to allow redevelopment of their Parkhead home, John Collins was the club's top league scorer with only eight goals.

— ARTISTIC SUPPORT —

Public figures have never tended to be shy of confessing their affection for Celtic. As former Creation Records mogul and one-time manager of Oasis Alan McGee said "Celtic have all the cool people supporting them and Rangers have me and Wet Wet Wet!" Celtic's celeb backers include:

Actors
Peter Mullan
James McAvoy
Henry Cusick
Jennifer Love Hewitt
Ashley Judd
Tony Roper
Billy Connolly

Musicians
Fran Healy
Sharleen Spiterri
Paolo Nuttini
The Fratellis
Rod Stewart
Clare Grogan
Jim Kerr
Shane McGowan
Mogwai
Primal Scream
Saw Doctors
Westlife

Sportspeople
Frank 'the Chief' Banham (ice hockey)
Dario Franchitti (racing)
Eddie Jordan (racing)
Lawrence Tynes (American football)
Barry 'the bizness' Morrison (boxing)
John Higgins (snooker)
Alan McManus (snooker)
Paul McGinley (golf)

Damien Duff (football)

Maybes aye, maybes no
Martin Scoresese
Mickey Rourke
Hulk Hogan
Jay-Z
Snoop-Dog
Leylani Lei (Asian porn star)
Martine McCutcheon
Bono
Oasis
Arctic Monkeys
Tony Hadley
Wayne Rooney
Roy Keane

Dyke-jumper (from Celtic to Rangers)
Sean Connery

Others
Dominik Diamond (but Celtic supporters don't like to talk about
him)

— ANOTHER NAME FOR CELTIC —

The team itself is often referred to as the Celts, the Hoops or the
Tic, for reasons that are plain. 'The Bhoys' is also popular, a nod
to the club's Irish identity with the 'h' added for the name to sound
as it would delivered by those across the water. An oft-heard name
given to the side in 1970s was the Pope's XI, a tongue-in-cheek term
alluding to Celtic's Catholic origins.

'The Tims' remains a well-used expression to denote both the
club and their supporters. Various reasons have been forwarded.
One is that Tim Malloy was the generic name given to Irish Catholic
immigrants. Another is that it is rhyming slang for Bhoys. A more
sinister suggestion is that it is because Tim Malloy was the name
of a 1920s Glasgow razor gang who tended to reserve their blade-
flashing for Protestant rivals.

— CELTIC LEGENDS: DANNY McGRAIN —

Danny McGrain: the brilliant, marauding defender

Longevity, unerring excellence and fortitude are each in themselves hallmarks of greatness. In Danny McGrain's Celtic career, the three become one. Across the early 1970s it was accepted as fact that the right-back was the finest exponent of the overlapping style in world football. What's more, it is doubtful if there have been many more courageous players than the affable Glaswegian.

Three times McGrain suffered potentially career-crushing setbacks. In 1972 he sustained a fractured skull against Falkirk, just as he was edging his way into the senior set-up. The injury merely delayed that permanent graduation by six months. More challengingly, he was diagnosed with diabetes in 1974, at a time when managing the illness was considered at odds with athletic pursuit. McGrain proved that was otherwise. Indeed, it was inspirational to other sufferers that he continued to develop as a maurading defender, wedding speed and stamina to poise and control. At least until, as recently appointed captain, he suffered a seemingly innocuous ankle injury in October 1977. The problem kept medics baffled over how to define it or treat it and sidelined McGrain for over a year. He later admitted that there were many times during this lay-off that he thought he was never coming back.

He returned a more deliberate defender, who had to choose his moments in attack with his pace dulled. But, as before, he remained a composed, bedrock figure in Celtic's winning moments. At 36, he was key in the inconceivable last-day title success delivered by a 5–0 win over St Mirren at Love Street in May 1986.

That was fully 19 years after he had joined the club, a short time after a scout from Rangers passed up the opportunity to sign him believing that, as Danny Fergus McGrain, he must be a Catholic. In fact, he was a Rangers-supporting Protestant. McGrain was the only member of Celtic's fabled 'Quality Street Kids', comprising Kenny Dalglish, Lou Macari, David Hay and George Connelly, to devote his best years to the club. He did so as an always approachable, willing professional who would have gained more Scotland caps than the then Celtic record of 62 but for injury.

McGrain's importance to the Scottish team can be measured by the fact that the calamitious 1978 World Cup finals campaign in Argentina was, in part, attributed to his enforced absence. It was even immortalised in Rod Stewart's questionable ditty, *Ole Ola*, which contained the line "I only wish we had Danny McGrain".

McGrain felt wounded that he was not afforded a proper send-off on being released in 1987, after which he had a month as player–coach with Rochdale Rovers in Brisbane before joining Hamilton Academical. Spells coaching at Clydebank and in Zambia followed, before a stint as manager of Arbroath. He returned to Celtic's backroom set-up in the 1990s and is currently assistant reserve coach.

Danny McGrain factfile
Born: Glasgow, 1st May 1950
Appearances: 663
Goals: 7
Full international appearances while at Celtic: 62 caps for
Scotland
Honours:
League championship: 1972/73, 1973/74, 1976/77, 1978/79,
1980/81, 1981/82, 1985/86
Scottish Cup: 1974, 1975, 1977, 1980, 1985
League Cup: 1974/75, 1982/83

— SPLASHING THE CASH —

Celtic's ten most expensive purchases (although some figures have
since been disputed):

Fee	Player	Signed from	Date
£6m	Chris Sutton	Chelsea	July 2000
£6m	John Hartson	Coventry City	July 2001
£5.75m	Eyal Berkovic	West Ham	July 1999
£5.75m	Neil Lennon	Leicester City	December 2000
£4.7m	Rafael Scheidt	Corithians	December 1999
£4.4m	Scott Brown	Hibernian	July 2007
£3.75m	Joos Valgaeren	Roda	July 2000
£3.4m	Jan Vennegoor of Hesselink	PSV Eindhoven	August 2006
£3m	Massimo Donati	AC Milan	July 2007
£2.75m	Alan Thompson	Aston Villa	September 2000

— SUNDAY SCORING SERVICE —

Dixie Deans scored the first ever competitive goal on a Sunday in
Scotland, in a 6–1 home win over Clydebank on 27th January
1974. Deans went on to score the first ever Sunday hat-trick that
same day.

— HULLO, HULLO, IT'S NOT THE
SONG YOU KNOW —

The old American Civil War anthem *Marching through Georgia* is forever associated with Rangers. It is the source of *The Billy Boys*, a song that led to the Ibrox club being fined by UEFA in 2006 for 'discriminatory chanting' at the Champions League tie away to Villareal because of the line "up to our knees in Fenian blood". *Fenian*, in this context, stands for Catholic. They were the enemies of the Billy Boys, a Glasgow razor gang led by former British Fascists member Billy Fullerton, who enjoyed their heyday in the 1930s.

However, *Marching through Georgia* originally formed the basis for a Celtic song, sung by supporters keen to rhapsodise about a 5–0 mauling of Rangers in the semi-final of the Scottish Cup in March 1925. They did so with choice language:

> *Hullo, Hullo*
> *We are the Tim Malloys*
> *Hello, Hullo*
> *You'll know us by our noise*
> *We f*** the Rangers in the cup,*
> *It was good to be alive*
> *Not one, not two, not three, not four but five*

— GREEN-AND-WHITE CHRISTMAS —

Celtic have played 15 matches on Christmas Day, winning 13, drawing one and losing one.

— TRAINED FOR TEN MEN —

On 24th January 1891 Celtic played a whole match with ten men after Mick McKeown missed the train for the game against Vale of Leven. They lost 3–1.

— UNFORGETTABLE GAMES:
TEN MEN WON THE LEAGUE —

Celtic 4 Rangers 2, Premier Division, Celtic Park, 21st May 1979

"Singing, ten men won the league . . . tra la la lala" was the chant that resounded whenever Celtic supporters gathered throughout the summer of 1979. It followed an all-time classic backs-to-the-wall title clincher against, most satisfyingly of all, their greatest rivals.

On a Monday night, Rangers travelled to the East End of Glasgow for a postponed fixture knowing they only had to avoid defeat to be virtually certain of claiming the championship. Celtic, unexpectedly turned around in only a matter of months by new manager Billy McNeill, had performed minor miracles to remain in contention. A fixture pile-up following a bitter winter meant they played only one league game in three months.

By the 55th minute of this league decider major miracles were required of them. Trailing to an early Alex MacDonald goal, a petulant kick by Celtic winger Johnny Doyle reduced the home side to ten men. However the sending off, while apparently sounding the death knell for Celtic's title hopes, instead energised McNeill's men. Goals from Roy Aitken and George McCluskey put Celtic 2–1 up before a 74th-minute effort from Bobby Russell levelled the scores.

But Celtic were not to be denied and pressed on confidently. With five minutes remaining, their pressure paid off when Colin Jackson headed into his own net. Then, only seconds from the end, Murdo MacLeod, with a shot to nothing from 25 yards, rocketed the ball into the top corner for a victory that was celebrated with greater fervour than any since the Lisbon Lions era.

"There's a fairytale aspect of Celtic which shows itself every now and again," said McNeill. "That was another of our wee tales that will be remembered as long as anyone is alive who was there".

Celtic: Latchford, McGrain, Lynch, Aitken, McAdam, Edvaldsson, Provan, Conroy (Lennox), McCluskey, MacLeod, Doyle
Rangers: McCloy, Jardine, Dawson, Johnstone, Jackson, MacDonald, McLean (Miller), Russell, Parlane, Smith, Cooper

— THE FIELDS OF ATHENRY —

If ever a song chimed in with Celtic's orgins, it is *The Fields of Athenry*. Written by Pete St John in 1981, it tells the story of a young man, Michael, who is banished to Australia for stealing corn to feed his family during Ireland's potato famine of the mid-1880s. Although those Irish immigrants who founded Celtic were not forcibly removed from their homeland, the same famine compelled them to resettle in Glasgow. They experienced exactly the same sense of loss and dislocation evoked in the ballad.

Why the song became Celtic's unofficial anthem in the mid-1990s is a matter for debate. Chris Morris, Republic of Ireland international and Celtic full-back between 1987 and 1992, claims he deserves credit. In an interview in 1998 he said he heard the song on international trips, started to sing it as his party piece at Celtic supporters' clubs functions, and it took hold from there.

By a lonely prison wall
I heard a young girl calling
Micheal they have taken you away
For you stole Trevelyn's corn
So the young might see the morn
Now a prison ship lies waiting in the bay

Low lie the fields of Athenry
Where once we watched the small free birds fly.
Our love was on the wing
we had dreams and songs to sing
It's so lonely round the fields of Athenry

By a lonely prison wall
I heard a young man calling
Nothing matter Mary when your free,
Against the Famine and the Crown
I rebelled they cut me down
Now you must raise our child with dignity

Low lie the fields of Athenry
Where once we watched the small free birds fly.
Our love was on the wing

we had dreams and songs to sing
It's so lonely round the fields of Athenry

By a lonely harbour wall
She watched the last star falling
As that prison ship sailed out against the sky
Sure she'll wait and hope and pray
For her love in Botany Bay
It's so lonely round the fields of Athenry

Low lie the fields of Athenry
Where once we watched the small free birds fly.
Our love was on the wing
we had dreams and songs to sing
It's so lonely round the fields of Athenry

— TROPHIES WON: DECADE BY DECADE —

	League	Scottish Cup	League Cup	Europe	Total
1880s	0	0	0	0	0
1890s	4	2	0	0	6
1900s	5	4	0	0	9
1910s	6	3	0	0	9
1920s	2	3	0	0	5
1930s	2	3	0	0	5
1940s	0	0	0	0	0
1950s	1	2	2	0	5
1960s	4	3	5	1	13
1970s	7	5	1	0	13
1980s	4	4	1	0	9
1990s	1	1	1	0	3
2000s	6	4	14	0	14

— UNFORGETTABLE GAMES:
MIRACLE ON LOVE STREET —

St Mirren 0 Celtic, 5, Premier Division, Love Street, 3rd May 1986

Like the Sex Pistols concert at the 100 Club, every Celtic supporter of a certain vintage claims to have been at Love Street on the final day of the 1985/86 season still believing the nigh impossible could happen.

A 16-game league unbeaten run – the last eight of these won – allowed Celtic to stay on the tails of Hearts, at the Premier Division summit throughout the second half of that season. But the feeling pre-match was that the best chance of a monumental upset had gone when Davie Hay's men only beat Motherwell 2–0 four days earlier.

That result meant that, for a dramatic flip, Celtic had to secure a three-goal victory over St Mirren while the Edinburgh club lost at Dundee. The chances of the second part of the equation happening seemed remote, as Hearts were on a 31-game unbeaten run that had taken them to within touching distance of a league and Scottish Cup double.

Everything changed at precisely 4.25pm that afternoon. And in this most extraordinary of outcomes, the man remembered as Celtic's defining hero wasn't wearing the famous hoops at all, although he was a rabid supporter. He was Dundee player Albert Kidd, whose goals against Hearts as a substitute snatched the championship from the Tynecastle men's grasp.

Meanwhile, Celtic were 5–0 up, having ruthlessly dismantled their hosts with breathtaking attacking football that brought goals from Brian McClair, and a double from Mo Johnston inside 32 minutes.

Celtic's rapid reaching of the necessary winning margin made for the oddest scenes at Love Street from that point on. Paul McStay and McClair added strikes either side of the interval, but these goals only raised muted cheers among the visiting supporters, most of whom were more concerned about following events at Dundee on their radios. Kidd's opener seven minutes from time brought an eruption on the Love Street terraces. His second, a minute later, sparked pandemonium as Celtic's legions celebrated perhaps their most remarkable title success, and ended a four-year wait for the championship.

The final whistle was the cue for a mass pitch invasion, euphoric fans smothering the Celtic players. Kidd's vital role in one of the club's most legendary days was not forgotten, with one supporters' club for a while bearing his name.

St Mirren: Stewart, Wilson, D Hamilton, B Hamilton, Godfrey, Cooper, Fitzpatrick, Abercromby, McGarvey, Gallagher (Speirs), Mackie
Celtic: Bonner, McGrain (Grant), Whyte, Aitken, McGugan, MacLeod, McClair, P McStay, Johnston, Burns, Archdeacon

— VEGA'S BRACE —

Swiss centre back Ramon Vega holds the distinction of being the last Celtic debutant to net a double. A loan signing from Tottenham Hotspur, he achieved the feat in a 6–0 home thrashing of Aberdeen on 16th December 2000.

— ALL IN —

The last outfield Celtic player to play every match (league, League Cup, Scottish Cup and Europe) in a season was Chris Morris back in 1987/88. In 2005/06, Neil Lennon and John Hartson played in every league match but not all the cup ties.

— SEATS FOR SCRIBES —

In 1894, it is believed that the first ever press box installed at a football ground anywhere in the world opened at Celtic Park.

— ALL WE ARE SAYING, IS GIVE US TWO-IN-A-ROW —

In 1959 Celtic played 38 league matches and did not win two in a row.

— PLAYER OF THE YEAR —

Celtic players to have won major individual awards:

Scottish Football Writers' Association award (inaugurated 1965):

1965 Billy McNeill
1967 Ronnie Simpson
1969 Bobby Murdoch
1973 George Connelly
1977 Danny McGrain
1983 Charlie Nicholas
1987 Brian McClair
1988 Paul McStay
1998 Craig Burley
1999 Henrik Larsson
2001 Henrik Larsson
2002 Paul Lambert
2004 Jackie McNamara
2005 John Hartson (shared with Fernando Ricksen of Rangers)
2007 Shunsuke Nakamura
2009 Gary Caldwell

Scottish Professional Footballers' Association award (inaugurated 1978):

1980 Davie Provan
1983 Charlie Nicholas
1987 Brian McClair
1988 Paul McStay
1991 Paul Elliott
1997 Paolo Di Canio
1998 Jackie McNamara
1999 Henrik Larsson
2000 Mark Viduka
2001 Henrik Larsson
2004 Chris Sutton
2006 Shaun Maloney
2007 Shunsuke Nakamura
2008 Aiden McGeady
2009 Scott Brown

— BROTHER WALFRID —

Brother Walfrid: Celtic founder

Celtic's founder Brother Walfrid was born Andrew Kerins in Ballymote, County Sligo on 18th May 1840. Information about his childhood is scarce but his early days were doubtless blighted by the potato famine (1845–52), which caused the deaths of a quarter of the Irish population. Kerins, like many of his contemporaries, contributed to the growing Irish diaspora in Scotland, arriving in Glasgow on a coal boat in 1855. He was never to return to Ireland.

Conditions in the Empire's second city were scarcely an improvement. Social deprivation was rife and most of the working poor lived in slums, while the Irish Catholic immigrant community also faced prejudice.

In the city's East End the Marist brothers were committed to providing education for workers and Kerins took full advantage of this opportunity, attending night classes to train as a teacher. Inspired by the Marists' ethos he became a monk in 1864, undergoing his training at Beauchamp in France. He returned to Glasgow, as Brother Walfrid, in 1868 and began teaching in St Mary's School. By 1874 he had been promoted to headmaster of the Sacred Heart School, also in Glasgow's East End. In an effort to alleviate poverty Walfrid and his colleague Brother Dorotheus, together with the St Vincent De Paul Society, founded a charity called the Poor Children's Dinner Table. The Penny Dinners, as they were better known, fed the children of the neighbourhood and by charging a penny allowed parents to 'save face', as Brother Dorotheus put it, in not appearing to rely on charity. In fact, Walfrid suggested that parents who only had a halfpenny could supply their own bread.

Charity on such a scale required fundraising. The astute Walfrid saw the perfect opportunity when he arranged a match between Catholic club Edinburgh Hibernian and Renton, an event that attracted 15,000 paying spectators. Following the now famous celebrations after Hibernian's Scottish Cup win in 1887, Walfrid began planning a similar team for Glasgow's East End. The formation of Celtic though, was not just about charity. Walfrid, and the Archdiocese, were keen to thwart the Presbyterian Church's attempts to recruit Catholic members with their own soup kitchens.

Celtic would also offer a much-needed cultural focus for these Irish immigrants. Edinburgh Hibernian's win, and the subsequent celebrations in Glasgow, had shown Walfrid the powerful need for the community to have its own identity.

The football club's formation was made possible by Walfrid's charisma. As well as vision and purpose, he had a network of contacts that he used to the full. "A wonderful organising power, of lovable nature and a man who only had to knock and it was opened," is how he was described by early Celt Tom Maley.

It was perhaps Walfrid's success in Glasgow that prompted his superiors to send him to London to work with the poor in Bow and

Bethnal Green in 1892. He contemplated the formation of a 'London Celtic' but realised that the geographical spread of the Irish immigrant community in the capital made it unfeasible, though he is believed to have organised matches between local children.

His work in London ended in 1908 and his final assignment for the Marists was to found a home teaching college in Canterbury to replace the French school at Beauchamp. He died on 17th April 1915 and is buried in the grounds of St Joseph's College, Dumfries.

In 2005, a bronze statue of Walfrid, paid for by supporters, was placed at the front entrance of the club's stadium.

— FRANK OF ALL TRADES —

No individual has served Celtic in more capacities across the football domain than Frank Connor. After being on the books as a goalkeeper between 1960 and 1962, the Blantyre-born Connor returned as youth coach in the late 1970s. In between various spells managing elsewhere, he later came back to Parkhead as Celtic assistant manager and first team coach.

However, he will always be remembered for stepping into the breach and holding the senior side together following the resignations of manager Liam Brady and his assistant Joe Jordan within 24 hours in early October 1993. In fact, he is fondly referred to as Celtic's only unbeaten manager. When Lou Macari was appointed later that month, just before an Old Firm game, he allowed the caretaker to lead the team out at Ibrox. A fighting victory ensued. Connor then settled into the post of reserve team coach before he had a spell as kitman.

Connor's record as manager:

Date	Result
9th Oct 1993	Celtic 2 Dundee 1
16th Oct 1993	Hibernian 1 Celtic 1
20th Oct 1993	Celtic 1 Sporting Lisbon 0 (UEFA Cup)
30th Oct 1993	Rangers 1 Celtic 2

— OLD FIRM NIGHTMARE —

Celtic suffered their worst Old Firm defeat for 95 years when they were thrashed 5–1 at Ibrox on 17th August 1988. The centenary double of only months before seemed a distant memory as Celtic were battered by Rangers, who romped to their biggest derby win since 1893.

It could have been worse, too, as Celtic found themselves 5–1 down with half an hour to play. "I was praying it wasn't going to go to seven," Tommy Burns said afterwards (a reference to Celtic's famous 7–1 derby victory). The heavy defeat set the tone for a comfortable title success for the Ibrox men.

— ALL SCOTS AND YET NOT —

Celtic last fielded a starting XI comprised entirely of Scotland nationals on 3rd December 1994. It will probably never happen again. But you could nitpick. All the players Tommy Burns selected for the club's league game that day were eligible to play for Scotland. But midfielder Stuart Gray, son of famous international Eddie Gray, was born in Harrogate, though he did represent Scotland under-21s.

The 'home' side didn't do Celtic much good in their temporary Hampden abode. They could only draw 2–2 against Motherwell, despite taking a 2–0 lead. They were pegged back by a double from former Celt Tommy Coyne, a Republic of Ireland international born in Scotland.

Celtic's all Scottish XI: Marshall, Boyd, McKinlay, Galloway, O'Neil, Grant, McLaughlin (Donnelly), McStay, Falconer, Walker, Gray

— DROPPED FOR ONLY SCORING FOUR —

How many players are dropped after netting a quartet of goals? On 24th September 1983, Brian McClair scored four times in a 6–2 league win against Dundee at Dens Park but was replaced by Jim Melrose for the next match four days later. However, Celtic manager Davie Hay did not have cause to rue that decision. His team won 4–1 away to Aarhus of Denmark in the second leg of their UEFA Cup first-round tie.

— SHORT AND THE LONG OF IT —

It is difficult to be definitive over the diminutive when it comes to Celtic's shorties. Heights records are unreliable from the early days and, indeed, as recently as the 1960s. But, fittingly, 'Wee Willie' Crilly, a 5ft 3in 1920s centre forward, appears to win the contest by an inch from famous 1950s midfielder Bobby Collins, and early 1990s winger Brian McLaughlin.

There appears less doubt about the tallest Celtic players. Defender Ian McWilliams, who played four games for the club in 1977/78, measured up to 6ft 5in, without his boots on, as did Stanislav Varga, a central defender with the club from 2003 to 2006.

— AND BOYD DOESN'T SCORE! —

In a Celtic career spanning 11 years following his move from Chelsea in February 1992, Tom Boyd scored just two goals in over 300 games. Both came in the league, the first away to St Mirren on 8th April 1992, the second away to Falkirk on 29th April 1995. The only goal he scored at Celtic Park was near the end of his days with Motherwell, in a 2–1 win for the Lanarkshire side on 30th March 1991. That was, in fact, his last goal for them. The Scotland international did however score a famous World Cup goal in the opening game of France 98 . . . for Brazil.

— CAN YOU HEAR US, 5 LIVE? —

On 1st April 1996, Jorge Cadete came on as a substitute for his debut and scored in a 5–0 league win over Aberdeen. The roar to greet the Portuguese striker's effort was so loud that BBC Radio 5 Live, covering the match, lost transmission for 15 seconds.

— LONG IBROX WAIT ENDS —

When Celtic beat Rangers 3–2 at Ibrox on 21st September 1957 it was their first derby win at the ground in 22 years.

— UNFORGETTABLE MATCHES: THE DAY IT ALL CHANGED —

Celtic 6 Rangers 2, league, Celtic Park, 27th August 2000

Some games change everything. One such occasion was Martin O'Neill's first Old Firm game – or the Demolition Derby as it is now more commonly know by Celtic supporters, who probably still occasionally put on the DVD of their team's most emphatic league victory over their rivals.

O'Neill had already raised Celtic spirits when his side welcomed Rangers to their backyard for the fifth game of the 2000/01 season. In the early weeks of his first campaign, O'Neill had restored confidence to a team that had become drained of that quality as they finished a record 21 points behind Dick Advocaat's men the previous season.

But Rangers represented the ultimate test and headed into the latest city skirmish unbeaten in their previous seven derbies. Both teams had warmed up for the encounter with four straight league wins but, on a sunny afternoon in Glasgow's East End, O'Neill's team sizzled and their opponents melted.

Amazingly, Celtic were 3–0 up before 13 minutes had passed, their first goal arriving after only a minute and in fortunate circumstances when recent £6m arrival Chris Sutton touched in a Henrik Larsson shot when marginally offside.

With Rangers right-back Fernando Ricksen performing like a frightened kitten against winger Bobby Petta – the defender was hooked before the half was out – and his teammates overpowered by their rivals' O'Neill-inspired drive and hunger, the atmosphere at Celtic Park was off the richter scale. It even went up a notch higher when Stilian Petrov headed in a second before Paul Lambert added a third.

Strangely, after such a sensational start, Celtic's play then became rather untidy. Rangers gradually recovered their composure and looked capable of making go of it, especially after Claudio Reyna pulled a goal back. Rod Wallace then had a strike wrongly ruled out for offside and the half-time break came as a welcome relief for Celtic.

They returned after the break in much better shape. Larsson, who previously looked out of sorts, was now operating on a different plain. He produced the afternoon's most glorious moment, and one of his finest goals, when he nutmegged Bert Konterman and then delightfully chipped the advancing Rangers keeper. His near-post nod then made it 5–2 after Billy Dodds had pulled a goal back, and the game was over as a contest. There was still time, though, for Barry Ferguson to be sent off for a second bookable offence before Sutton fired in a sixth in the last minute.

The events of the afternoon proved to be pivotal to Celtic's domination of the Scottish scene, and had a psychological influence on Old Firm encounters throughout the early years of the new millennium. Most importantly, the fact that all but two of the home performers that day had been at Celtic Park prior to O'Neill's arrival graphically demonstrated that the new manager had a precious ability to instill a ruthless winning mentality in his players.

Celtic: Gould, Stubbs, Valgaeren, Mahe, McNamara, Moravcik (Boyd), Lambert (Mjallby), Petrov, Petta, Larsson (Burchill), Sutton
Rangers: Klos, Ricksen (Tugay), Amoruso, Konterman, Vidmar (Kanchelskis), Reyna, Ferguson, van Bronckhorst, McCann (Loven krands), Dodds, Wallace

— GREATEST EVER CELTIC TEAM —

In 2002 Celtic fans voted for the club's best ever team. Understandably perhaps, the Lisbon Lions dominate, with seven of those who played in the 1967 European Cup triumph making the starting XI:

1. Ronnie Simpson
2. Danny McGrain
3. Tommy Gemmell
4. Bobby Murdoch
5. Billy McNeill
6. Paul McStay
7. Jimmy Johnstone
8. Bertie Auld
9. Henrik Larsson
10. Kenny Dalglish
11. Bobby Lennox

— PLAIN, STRIPES AND HOOPS —

Celtic had been in existence for some 14 years before the club hit upon the idea of kitting out the team in a green-and-white hooped shirt and white shorts. So it was that in 1903/04 one of the classically distinctive football strips of world football, and a design indelibly associated with the club and its teams, was born. It debuted on 29th August 1903 in a 3–1 defeat by Third Lanark.

- A commonly used strip in the early days was green-and-white vertical stripes with dark-blue serge pants. One early incarnation of Celtic's on-field colours even featured the unthinkable . . . blue.

- The strip worn in the club's very first match on 28th May 1888 was a white shirt with green collar and a Celtic cross on the left breast.

- A club crest did not feature on the hoops, modified only as much as collars and button-up fronts coming and going with fashion trends, until the 1977/78 season. Then a four-leaf clover – a good-luck symbol allegedly found in the first sod of turf laid at the new Celtic Park of 1892 – featured in a circular badge with 'The Celtic Football and Athletic Co.'. It was placed in the middle of a hooped shirt with white v-neck collar.

- Only in one season since has the four-leaf clover not been present. To mark the club's 1987/88 centenary season the crest on the strip once more became a Celtic cross.

- One of Fergus McCann's bright ideas as new owner in 1994 was to change the badge to incorporate a thistle, making more of Celtic's Scottish identity. Mercifully, the thistle never took root.

- Crimes against both tradition and fashion were committed by the club in their strips of the 1990s. In 1993 the hoops gave way to huge eye-sore bands and in 1995 Umbro produced a shirt which had combination of fat and thin hoops – and we're not even started on the change kits (See *Away with the Fairies*, page 132). Then, in 2001, the hoops were broken with gaps under the arms. Supporters deemed such meddling with their cherished colours unacceptable.

— McCANN'S THE (MISUNDERSTOOD) MAN —

Fergus McCann, quite simply, is the father of the modern-day Celtic. Without his transformation of the club that followed his 1994 takeover, Celtic would not be the dominant team of the Scottish game, a credible European force and playing in front of 60,000 crowds at one of the most celebrated sporting amphitheatres in world football.

After nearly 100 years of dynastical control, Celtic were on the brink of bankruptcy when McCann embarked on a five-year plan after acquiring 51 per cent of the club's shares and assuming responsibility for the club's £7m debt in February 1994. It followed a long battle for control in which the irascible Scots-Canadian was the man with the money in the 'rebel' group, and camera-friendly Glasgow businessman Brian Dempsey the populist figurehead.

McCann eventually made good on every one of the key elements of his business model without Dempsey, who was sidelined after failing to stump up his previously agreed contribution to the club's recapitalisation.

From the start, there were suspicions about the motives of a man for whom every penny was a prisoner. But McCann's obsession with the bottom line was, equally, a refusal to threaten the club's financial stability. His determination to follow his principles, whether on fiscal or social matters, brought him into conflict with a cast of thousands. In 1996 he introduced the Bhoys Against Bigotry campaign to rid the club of a sectarian streak he believed found its expression in chants sung by "Catholic bigots" that invoked the IRA or had religious overtones.

Famously, he brought down SFA chief executive Jim Farry after Jorge Cadette was prevented from featuring in the 1996 Scottish Cup semi-final because the governing body unnecessarily delayed his registration. McCann pursued the matter for two years before Farry was forced to resign when it emerged there had been administrative errors.

Despite victories like that, McCann never received more than grudging acceptance from Celtic's followers. It didn't help that he was an outsider, having made his money through a golf vacation company based in Montreal and Arizona. He ploughed half of his estimated £15m fortune into Celtic, and made a healthy return when he sold his holding for a £29m profit in 1999. McCann then fulfilled a promise to 'divest' his shares among supporters, although Dermot Desmond has since become the club's driving force with a 30 per cent stake.

Rather than adding to his fortune, McCann was motivated by a desire to restore Celtic to something like the status the club enjoyed when he was growing up in Croy, on the outskirts of Glasgow. "Don't people realise there are easier ways to make money?" he despaired of his critics.

However, his refusal to entertain football's speculate-to-accumulate philosophy – "it is all based on jam tomorrow!" he would sneer – put him in conflict with the club's supporters, who urged McCann to loosen the purse strings. For years league success proved elusive until new appointment Wim Jansen secured the title in 1998. McCann, though, was given no credit for that triumph, especially after Jansen resigned a mere two days afterwards claiming he could no longer work with the Celtic chairman or director of football Jock Brown, McCann's supposed henchman.

As a result, McCann was jeered when he unfurled the title flag at the first game the following season. A shameful moment in Celtic's history.

McCann has rarely spoken of his time at Celtic since returning to the other side of the Atlantic and making a success of a luxury bus service that ferries well-heeled businessmen between Boston and Manhatttan. Belatedly, though, Celtic fans are starting to acknowledge his achievements and legacy.

— KENNY SIGNS IN LINE —

Even at the height of his Celtic fame, Kenny Dalglish made time to sign countless autographs after home matches – on one proviso. Uncomfortable when crowded by eager fans, he would agree to sign for every supporter just so long as they stood in a single file line.

— THE FAR EAST END OF GLASGOW
FOURTH ESTATE —

From Tokyo to Tollcross was the cross-globe, culture shock-shift that Daisuke Nakajima opted for to follow Shunsuke Nakamura to the East End of Glasgow in the summer of 2005.

Nakajima was one of the handful of journalists from his homeland who had devoted their lives to covering every cough, spit and burp of the Far East's most high-profile footballer in the four years he spent in Glasgow.

A popular figure around the club, the amiable Nakajima describes it as simply the Japanese way to report obsessively on their major sporting figures. The capacity for producing lighter moments is not lost on him. Once asked if he still produced match reports for Celtic games in which Nakamura didn't play, he replied: "No, I file the scoreline . . . and that he didn't play."

— KENNY'S FINAL GOAL —

He will have little to reflect on ruefully from his days displaying his extraordinary talents at Celtic in the 1970s, but Kenny Dalglish might wish he had scored in fewer finals for the club. On every occasion he did, Celtic lost:

Date	Competition	Result
23rd Oct 1971	League Cup	Celtic 1 Partick Thistle 4
9th Dec 1972	League Cup	Celtic 1 Hibernian 2
5th May 1973	Scottish Cup	Celtic 2 Rangers 3
6th Nov 1976	League Cup	Celtic 1 Aberdeen 2

— THE BIGGEST SPENDERS —

Celtic have broken the record transfer fee paid by a Scottish club on just three occasions in the modern era:

Date	Player	Signed from	Fee
11th Oct 1984	Mo Johnston	Watford	£440,000
8th July 1999	Eyal Berkovic	West Ham United	£5.75m
11th July 2000	Chris Sutton	Chelsea	£6m

— OSSIE THINKS HE'S DREAMING —

As he sprinted out of the Celtic Park tunnel in Tottenham Hotspur colours for a pre-season friendly in Glasgow on 16th August 1983, Ossie Ardiles was entitled to feel apprehensive. The Argentine had missed most of the previous season with the White Hart Lane club after staying away from the UK in the aftermath of the Falklands War.

On his return to London six months later, he found himself remorselessly barracked at every away ground. Not Celtic, though. He was given a hero's reception by the home fans as he appeared on the field that day, the rousing nature of which left him utterly mystified. It is not known if any player in the home ranks took time to attempt to explain the Celtic support's contempt for the British establishment.

— SECOND BEST IN SECOND FINAL —

On 6th May 1970 Celtic missed a chance to win a second European Cup and cement their status as one of the continent's great sides when they lost to Feyenoord in the final in Milan.

Squabbles over bonus payments and strangely slipshod preparation from Jock Stein contributed to a disappointing showing. Celtic played nothing like the team who only three weeks earlier had dismantled Leeds United. And though they took an early lead through Tommy Gemmell, they could have no real complaints about a 2–1 defeat after extra time.

— GOING DOWN WITH THE GOOD SHIP —

Celtic's hope of retaining the European Cup were effectively sunk the day the Queen Elizabeth II was launched from the Upper Clyde Shipyards in Clydebank on the afternoon of 20th September 1967.

That night in Glasgow, Dynamo Kiev inflicted a 2–1 defeat on the strangely out of sorts European champions. Despite battling manfully, Celtic could not retrieve the tie in Ukraine, drawing the second leg 1–1.

— CELTIC LEGENDS: BOBBY MURDOCH —

Bobby Murdoch: the complete footballer

"As far as I am concerned, Murdoch was just about the best player I had as manager," said John Stein of the dynamic, powerful midfielder who starred in his legendary Lisbon Lions, Celtic's greatest ever team. No higher praise could have been offered to a sublimely gifted performer.

Yet, after watching his side effectively passed into submission in the 1967 European Cup Final by Murdoch, Inter Milan manager Helenio Herrara came close to providing an even greater eulogy. "My complete footballer," he said of the man whose talents Celtic came dangerously close to squandering.

Celtic signed Murdoch on schoolboy forms as a 15-year-old in 1959. Following a spell farmed out to Cambuslang Rangers, he was handed a debut in a League Cup win over Hearts in August 1962 that saw him net as an inside forward. But the abilities of the barrel-chested, but balletic, two-footer were not suited to the front line and in the trophyless years of 1963 and 1964, Celtic's faithful made it plain they had no faith in Murdoch as a main striker. Neither did the club, as he flitted in and out of the side as a fill-in for various attacking positions.

By 1964, Murdoch was giving serious thought to a new start in Australia with his young family. Stein's arrival as manager the following year allowed him to make his new start at Celtic, as a right half. Many consider this redeployment Stein's greatest masterstroke as Murdoch's pairing with Bertie Auld in the centre of the park provided Celtic with two formidable string-pullers.

Unfortunately, ankle and weight problems bothered Murdoch from the early years of his career. Just as he should have been reaching his peak in his late twenties, and after regular trips to health farms and an intensive training programme, he seemed to lose a little of his edge across his full set of attributes, which included scoring from range.

Murdoch's appetite also seemed to have waned and he claimed there was "no sense of challenge anymore" when he was moved to Middlesbrough in 1973. Before he retired in 1976 he produced some genuine Murdoch magic to help the club to promotion. He also played a role in the development of a young fellow Scot, Graeme Souness – later joking, "I sometimes wish I hadnae bothered," as Souness guided Rangers to title success. Murdoch became manager of Boro for an unhappy spell and did not enjoy the best fortune or health in his post-playing days. In 2001, he was the first Lion to die, after suffering a stroke.

Bobby Murdoch factfile
Born: Bothwell, Lanarkshire, 17th August 1944
Died: Glasgow, 15th May 2001
Appearances: 484
Goals: 102
Full international appearances while at Celtic: 12 caps for
Scotland
Honours:
League championship: 1965/66, 1966/67, 1967/68, 1968/69,
1969/70, 1970/71, 1971/72, 1972/73
Scottish Cup: 1965, 1967, 1969, 1972
League Cup: 1965/66, 1966/67, 1967/68, 1968/69, 1969/70
European Cup: 1967

— TOP CAPS —

Celtic's ten highest cap earners while with the club:

Name	Country	Years	Caps
1. Pat Bonner	Republic of Ireland	1981–96	80
2. Paul McStay	Scotland	1982–96	76
3. Tom Boyd	Scotland	1992–2001	66
4. Danny McGrain	Scotland	1973–82	62
5. Roy Aitken	Scotland	1979–89	50
6. Henrik Larsson	Sweden	1997–2004	49
7. Kenny Dalglish	Scotland	1971–77	47
8. Bobby Evans	Scotland	1948–60	45
9. Johan Mjallby	Sweden	1998–2004	40
10. John Collins	Scotland	1990–97	32

— THE REAL UNBEATABLES —

It is claimed of many teams that they are unbeatable. But it was
actually true of Willie Maley's Celtic, who were undefeated during
62 league games between 20th November 1915 and 14th April 1917.
The incredible sequence remains a British record.

— UNFORGETTABLE GAMES:
THE UNTHINKABLE AVOIDED —

Dundee 2 Celtic 3, league, Dens Park, 17th April 1948

It was considered desperate that a largely wet-behind-the-ears Celtic could only finish the 1946/47 season mid-table. Yet a year on, that placing smacked of respectability as a still-struggling young team came dangerously close to being responsible for Celtic slipping out of the top flight for the only time in their history.

It is incomprehensible to any supporter of the club under 60 that Celtic could flirt with relegation. But the drop was a very real threat in the build-up to their final league encounter of April 1948. As manager Jimmy McGrory later acknowledged in his autobiography: "I had the worst experience I ever had in football . . . It was with a heavy heart and a great deal of anxiety that we left Celtic Park for Dundee on April 17. On the way north I discussed the situation with our new chairman, Bob Kelly. I knew inwardly if Celtic had lost I would have to resign after only a couple of years [as manager]."

Celtic made the trip to Dens Park having dropped like a stone towards the relegation places in the weeks leading up to a match potentially critical to their future. In two home games during the previous fortnight, they had lost 3–1 to Third Lanark and 4–2 to Hibernian. These reverses followed a 5–1 tanking away to Third Lanark, a defeat which provoked genuine fear that the club were caught in an irreversible downturn.

At Dens Park on that fateful afternoon, Celtic knew anything other than victory would leave them depending on favourable results in games involving fellow relegation-threatened sides that were to follow. A crowd of 31,000 turned up to Tayside, many of them from Glasgow. The away fans were given the opening they desired when Jock Weir, signed from Blackburn Rovers for £7,000 two months earlier, netted for the visitors after only 14 minutes. By the hour mark, though, Celtic were 2–1 down and facing disaster.

However, inspired by Bobby Evans in his first game at right half, Celtic managed to find another gear and equalised through Weir 23 minutes from time. As the clocked clicked past 88 minutes, Weir scrambled in his third and Celtic were safe. At full-time the players exchanged hearty embraces – not quite the done thing in the late 1940s, but understandable given the circumstances. The travelling supporters shared in the unconfined expressions of relief, forgetting for a few moments that the campaign had been one of utter failure and near catastrophe.

The season ended with Celtic 12th in a 16-team league, just four points above the relegation trapdoor. It might have been very different, however, had they not shut that door themselves.

Dundee: Brown, Follon, Irvine, Gallacher, Gray, Boyd, Gunn, Pattiloo, Stewart, Ewen, Mackay

Celtic: Miller, Hogg, Mallan, Evans, Corbett, McAuley, Weir, McPhail, Lavery, Gallacher, Paton

— LAST-DAY TITLE LOSS —

On 21st May 2005 Celtic supporters woke up to the news that Martin O'Neill would be stepping down to care for his ill wife. They were sure, though, that his last league game in charge – away to Motherwell – would bring him a fourth title in five years. With Celtic on top of the SPL table, a win was all that was needed to settle the title and make Rangers' result at Hibs an irrelevance.

Against all the odds, however, the game at Fir Park provided an outcome O'Neill has since admitted he will "never get over"; a view shared by the club's faithful. To this day they cannot understand how, after Chris Sutton put them 1–0 up after 25 minutes, they dramatically crumbled at the close. Motherwell striker Scott McDonald – a Celtic supporter and a title winner with the club three years later – scored in the 87th and 90th minutes to force the helicopter carrying the trophy to change direction and head for Easter Road, where Rangers' 1–0 win allowed them to pinch the title by a single point.

— ENOUGH TO MAKE YOUR HEARTS GO . . . —

Celtic's on-field miseries between the 1954/55 and 1960/61 seasons resulted in their average home attendances falling behind Hearts as well as Rangers. Indeed, in the early years of that sequence, Celtic were only the fourth best supported team in Scotland.

— LISBON SIDELINES —

- In 1967, Celtic completed a unique quadruple: European Cup, league championship, Scottish Cup and League Cup. The club also captured the Glasgow Cup, and reserve league and cup. Jock Stein joked that Celtic would have won the Derby too, but the racing authorities wouldn't let Bobby Lennox enter it.

- A myth has grown up that Celtic became the first club to win the European Cup with home-grown players. In fact, Real Madrid did the same the year before. Another myth is that Jock Stein ensured the Lions would remain unbeaten by never fielding that same side again. Actually he so did for the first round of their European Cup defence, in the first leg at home to Dynamo Kiev in September 1967. And they were beaten 2–1.

- Celtic defender John Clark has said it was a mark of Jock Stein, a Protestant, that he ensured a priest came to the team's Estoril headquarters on the day of the final to say mass for the Catholic members of his squad. The final fell on a holiday of obligation, the Feast of Corpus Christi.

- Jock Stein also arranged for representatives of the Marist Brothers, the order of club founder Brother Walfrid, to be guests of Celtic for the final.

- It had been agreed that Ronnie Simpson would go up to collect the cup but he was too emotional to do so.

- Ticket prices for the final ranged from £2 7s 6d (£2.37½) for the centre stand down to 10s (50p) for a terracing place behind the goals.

— PLAY IT AGAIN —

Between 1889/90 and 1951/52, Celtic did not lose a single cup replay.

— HIS TIME IN THE HOOPS WILL
NOT BE TELEVISED —

Giles 'Gil' Heron, father of jazz musician and agit-prop poet Gill Scott-Heron, whose best known song is the 1970s number *The Revolution Will Not Be Televised*, played five games at centre forward for Celtic in the 1951/52 season before thinking better of the climate.

Jamaican-born Heron, nicknamed the Black Arrow, was the first black player to play for the club. Making his home in Chicago, he came to the club's attention in Detroit during their North American tour of 1951. A man of many talents, he was a boxer and cricketer of some repute and also had two books of poetry published. He died in a Detroit nursing home in November 2008, aged 87 years.

— BONNIE CLYDE RUIN KEANO DEBUT —

When Roy Keane made his Celtic debut against First Division Clyde in a Scottish Cup third round tie at Broadwood on 9th January 2006, TV cameras rolled up from near and from far.

Against all expectations, what they were treated to was a young Clyde side that had been assembled through open trials the previous summer running the legs off Keane and his colleagues, who included new Chinese centre back Du Wei. At half-time the visitors found themselves fortunate to be only two goals down. Maciej Zurawski pulled a goal back late on but it was not enough on a day when Celtic were made to look football paupers against a Clyde team that cost coppers.

— CELTIC LEGENDS: JIMMY DELANEY —

Jimmy Delaney: idolised like few others

Matt Busby regarded his capture of Jimmy Delaney as the catalyst for Manchester United becoming the leading English team in the post-war period. Delaney is also the only man to gain FA Cup winners' medals in Scotland, England and Northern Ireland. Yet it says everything about the winger's unshakeable bond with Celtic that he looked on his post-Glasgow career as little more than a footnote.

"Although I played with many great clubs, I always took great pride in the fact that most people still remember me as Jimmy Delaney of Celtic," he said in an interview with club newspaper *The Celtic View* a few years before his death in 1989. In the same article he recalled a Celtic jersey being interred with early player Tom Maley at his funeral and said, "I hope someone does that for me."

Delaney's ball-playing skills, speed off the mark and finishing power made him a performer idolised like few others in Celtic's history. He quickly became the focal point of one of the club's most prolific forward lines alongside Malcolm MacDonald, Johnny Crum, Jim Divers and Francis Murphy.

The rapid interplay between these five helped to deliver the championship in 1936, the Scottish Cup a year later and the Empire Exhibition trophy in 1938; the first of those successes arriving three years after the Cleland-born Delaney signed from Stoneyburn Juniors. In all he netted 73 goals in 160 peacetime games.

In part, he was beloved as much for his Corinthian approach to the game as for his monumental talents. "I doubt if there was ever a sportsman like Jimmy," was the tribute paid to him by tough-tackling Rangers captain Jock 'Tiger' Shaw. "When you took the ball away from him, you did so with the knowledge that you would never be tripped or pushed. I could have played against Delaney in my bare feet."

On 1st April 1939 Delaney suffered a gruesome arm fracture, the limb shattering so completely the surgeon treating him considered amputation. He returned two years later as the Second World War made football an ad hoc pursuit. A Scotland regular before his injury, in the years immediately afterwards the SFA would not select him for fear of being liable for crippling insurance pay-outs if he hurt the arm again.

Regular beatings by England and a public outcry brought his return in 1944. But by the time he popped up with the last-minute winner in a famous Victory International success in April 1946 he was a Manchester United player. A year before he had been dropped by Celtic because he had asked for an increase in his £2 a week wage and so began the long parting of the ways. Delaney proved to be a £4,000 bargain for Busby, reflected in the fact that he cost

Aberdeen £3,000 four-and-a-half years later, when he was 36. From Pittodrie, Delaney moved on to Falkirk, Derry City, Cork City and Elgin City as his career wound down.

"Jimmy was the greatest inspirational footballer I ever played with or saw. No game was ever lost with him in the team," suggested 1940s teammate Johnny Paton. Few Celtic supporters fortunate enough to have seen him would disagree.

Jimmy Delaney factfile
Born: Cleland, 3rd September 1914
Died: Cleland, 26th September 1989
Appearances: 160
Goals: 74
Full international appearances while at Celtic: 9 caps for Scotland
Honours:
League Championships: 1935/36, 1937/38
Scottish Cup: 1937
Empire Exhibition Trophy: 1938

— IT'S ALL GONE FOREIGN —

The first Celtic starting line-up for a competitive match not to feature either a Scottish-born player or a Scottish international came in the club's 114th year. On 8th September 2001 Celtic beat Dunfermline 3–1 with the following multi-national XI:

Player	Place of birth
Dimitri Kharine	Moscow (Russia)
Joos Valgaeren	Leuven (Belgium)
Didier Agathe	Saint-Pierre (Réunion)
Bobo Baldé	Marseille (France)
Olivier Tébily	Abidjan (Ivory Coast)
Alan Thompson	Newcastle (England)
Neil Lennon	Lurgan (Northern Ireland)
Stilian Petrov	Montana (Bulgaria)
Lubo Moravčík	Nitra (Slovakia)
Henrik Larsson	Helsingborg (Sweden)
Chris Sutton	Nottingham (England)

— JOCK STEIN OUT ON HIS OWN —

'The Big Man'

"I think he should have been a doctor or a psychologist," said Jimmy Johnstone of Jock Stein. "He knew people and because he knew what made us tick he made us feel we were the best team in the world. He knew how to make us believe in ourselves." In the context of Celtic, Stein was physician and shrink. He was also general, politician, life coach, talent spotter and orator. 'The Big Man', as he was known, is the colossus in a colossal Celtic history.

A miner in the Lanarkshire pits that also produced Matt Busby and Bill Shankly, Stein's success in guiding Celtic to nine consecutive titles was almost a by-product of his forging one of the most exhilarating teams to grace the European stage. For aside from the 1967 European Cup win which was his most celebrated achievement, he led Celtic to a final, two semi-finals and one quarter-final of the competition within an eight-year period. A grandmaster in tactical terms, part of his genius was in issuing his players with simple instructions. "He didn't fill our heads with wee motors," Billy Lennox said. But he turned a jalopy into a Formula One car when he was put behind the wheel at Celtic.

Yet, it is now accepted that this was transformation No 3 he effected at the club. Although he was once considered as simply an honest pro of a Celtic centre back in the 1950s, he is now recognised as possessing such leadership and motivational qualities that he was the driving force in the 1953/54 double side.

That the 'Kelly Kids' – the reserve side of the late 1950s named after the chairman Bob Kelly – later became his Lisbon Lions was also a consequence of Stein's work with them as reserve coach. His meticulous, modern, ballwork-focused coaching methods planted seeds. In 1960 Stein left to take over at Dunfermline because he felt he had "gone as far as he could" in not being a Catholic. When he returned on 8th March 1965, as the club's first non-Catholic manager and the first post-war to be given complete authority over team matters, he continued this work with his young charges, creating new life in a club that was in danger of withering permanently.

All the Lions except Willie Wallace were at the club when Stein returned. Players who had worked with him knew, as Billy McNeill commented, Celtic "would be different" with Stein at the helm. He had proved his powers to invigorate by turning Dunfermline from a near-demoted team to Scottish Cup winners – Celtic their 1962 final victims – and three times European entrants, before a short stint at Hibs ended while they were third in the table. Such was his thirst for football knowledge, in 1962 he was the only Scottish coach to attend a seminar at Lilleshall given by Gustav Sebes, the man behind the great Hungarian team of the 1950s who had destroyed England at Wembley, a game Stein had attended.

For his first training session at Celtic as manager, a squad used to running up and down the stadium's slopes were each given a ball. He gave them the confidence to use it artfully, having the precious ability to divine each player's greatest strengths, which for a number of the Lions meant slotting them into different berths. Under his stewardship there seemed no limit to how far Celtic could go. Though an incomparable man-manager, he ruled by fear in the dressing room and bullied press and referees to raise the standing of a club whose supporters he would wade into the stands to sort out if they were stepping out of line.

Combining old-school and new methods, Stein's crowning glory came in 1967, an all-conquering season capped by the European Cup win. The only blemish on his record followed in 1970 when he underestimated Feyenoord in his second European Cup Final.

He is said to have never properly recovered from a car accident in 1975 that almost claimed his life and kept him out of the game for a year. But even with his edge supposedly blunted he claimed a league and cup double on his return in 1976/77, to take his trophy haul at the club to 25. The team then disintegrated after losing Kenny Dalglish to Liverpool and Danny McGrain and Pat Stanton to injury. Finishing only fifth in the league and trophyless in 1978, his final campaign was a return to the sort of dismal days from which he saved the club.

Stein initially accepted an insulting offer to join the board as effectively a salesman, couched as a position "with a responsibility for fundraising", but left shortly afterwards to become manager of Leeds United. He lasted less than two months in the role before becoming Scotland manager.

He led his country to the World Cup finals in 1982 but on 10th September 1985 at Ninian Park in Cardiff, just after Scotland had scored a late penalty against Wales to put them into a play-off for the 1986 Mexico tournament, he suffered a massive heart attack and died 30 minutes later. He was mourned as he should have been, as a Scottish manager like no other, whose achievements the passing of time will never dim.

— CELTIC LEGENDS: PATSY GALLACHER —

The 'Mazy Meanderer'

Patsy Gallacher saved the very best in a Celtic career adorned by greatness to the very end. His last Scottish Cup final appearance in 1925 is now simply known by his name – 'the Patsy Gallacher Cup final' – because of the creation and execution of a goal that is one of the most famous in the club's history.

The equaliser from the little wing tormentor that hauled Celtic back on terms with 20 minutes remaining of their decider against Dundee on 11th April 1925 was recounted in all of its glory in the book *Alphabet of the Celts*: "He jinked, jouked, hurdled, swerved, dribbled, jumped, fell, got up, ran on, jinked again, stumbled, jouked once more, went over his wilkies [somersaulted] with the ball still grasped between his legs, and he was over the line, him and the ball, past an astonished Jock and Hampden to the last 75,000th man was rising in starry-eyed tribute to a genius in bootlaces. The momentum of the wee green devil meant he was caught in the net and had to be pulled out by his far-from-unhappy colleagues."

At only 5ft 6in, and seven stone in his early days, the Donegal-born 'Mazy Meanderer' (or 'Mighty Atom' or 'Tiny Bit o' Grit', as ran his other nicknames) wasn't supposed to be performing such feats a whole 14 years after he had joined the club from Clydebank Juniors. However undeniable were his wiles – he possessed ball control and dribbling and shooting power that could all be placed in the outrageous bracket – his fragile frame caused Celtic to hum and haw about recruiting him. As soon as they did, it became evident that his courage, nous and sheer will to win – by any means necessary – would offset any physique disadvantages.

Gallacher won over the hearts and minds of supporters immediately when making his debut against St Mirren in December 1911 and was an integral member of the four-in-a-row Celtic side of the 1910s. Luminaries who saw him play, such as Celtic chairman Bob Kelly and the club's greatest goalscorer Jimmy McGory, declared that Gallacher was without peer.

A player who recognised both his value and how capricious football could be, Gallacher insisted that Celtic allowed him to complete his apprenticeship as a shipwright before he signed a deal with them. As an established performer, he ensured he was given top wages and allowed to train in the afternoons so that he could look after his two pubs in the mornings. Moreover, when earning his first cap for Ireland against England at Belfast's Windsor Park, he became the highest paid international ever.

Gallacher's end at Celtic came when the club effectively retired him without his knowledge in July 1926. It was rumoured they did so to save on his hefty wage after a season during which he had struggled with knee problems. The fact he went on to play for six years with Falkirk gave the lie to Celtic's short-sighted assessment of a man declared at his funeral as "the greatest wee buggar that ever kicked a ba" by Rangers rival Tommy Cairns.

Patsy Gallacher factfile
Born: Ramelton, County Donegal, 16th April 1893
Died: Glasgow, 17th June 1953
Appearances: 464
Goals: 192
Full international appearances while at Celtic: 12 caps for
Ireland, 1 cap for the Irish Free State
Honours:
League championship: 1913/14, 1914/15, 1915/16, 1916/17,
1918/19, 1921/22
Scottish Cup: 1912, 1914, 1923, 1925

— HENRIK'S SPOT OF BOTHER —

Henrik Larsson didn't have an Achilles heel . . . except, perhaps,
when it came to converting penalties. During his seven years at the
club from 1997, he missed seven:

Date	Result
18th Aug 2001	Livingston 0 Celtic 0
30th Sept 2001	Rangers 0 Celtic 2
6th Dec 2001	Celtic 1 Valencia 0*
9th Feb 2002	Celtic 5 Dunfermline 0
14th Aug 2002	Celtic 3 Basel 1
10th April 2003	Celtic 1 Boavista 1

*Missed two (one in normal time, one in the penalty shoot-out).

— BHOY TO MAN —

Peter Wilson was but a slip of a lad when he made his Celtic debut
as an 18-year-old on 13th February 1924. So much so, the Ayrshire
right half was still dressing in short trousers when he met up with
his club colleagues in Glasgow to head out to Motherwell for his
first official match.

— CELTIC LEGENDS: PAUL McSTAY —

Paul McStay: Born to play for Celtic

The classic man out of time, Paul McStay's outstanding service to Celtic is not always recognised in the glowing terms it should be. That is for no other reason than the midfielder had the misfortune to play for the club through its darkest age of the modern era. In the trophy-bereft first half of the 1990s, he was often the only source of illumination.

Indeed, it was desperately cruel on a playmaker possessed of glorious technique and vision that, after 15 years turning in consistently exceptional performances, he was forced to retire aged 32 in 1997 – only a year before the club ended a decade without title success.

McStay was born to play for Celtic. The boy from the Rangers stronghold of Larkhall had Celtic in his genes as the great nephew of Celtic luminaries Jimmy and Willie McStay. A child prodigy, anyone who watched him even from his earliest youth knew he was destined for greatness. He first showed glimpses of his quality in Scotland colours, scoring twice in a memorable 5–4 defeat of England in a schoolboy international in 1980.

He also scored on his league debut against Aberdeen on 30th January 1982, a week after he made his first senior outing in the Scottish Cup against Queen of the South. That summer he captained Scotland to success in the UEFA Under-18s Championships before going on to make his full Scotland debut while still only 18.

Once described as "the pedigree player of Scottish football", although a diffident off-field character McStay was a dominant figure in all Celtic's 1980s success, thanks to his artful passing, drive and intelligence. The 1985 Scottish Cup final triumph was shared with his elder brother Willie, the first siblings to feature for the club in a cup win since their great uncles in 1927. Possibly, though, McStay enjoyed his career high-water mark when he wiped the board with the player-of-the-year honours after being the lynchpin of the club's league and Scottish Cup double in their 1987/88 centenary season.

Thereafter, Rangers' huge spend and Celtic's coinciding financial and talent drain led to McStay being denied a proper platform for his talents. He was unfairly burdened by being both captain, an honour bestowed on him after Roy Aitken left in January 1990, and the man of whom miracles were expected. He decided to leave in 1992, throwing his jersey into the the Jungle on the last day of a third consecutive trophyless season, but in the end thought better of offers from France and Italy and committed himself to the Celtic cause.

It was symptomatic of McStay's later years that, as Celtic sought to bring an end to more than five years without silverware, he should be the player to have his penalty saved in the earth-shattering shoot-out defeat by Raith Rovers in the final of the 1994 League

Cup. He recovered, though, to lead the club to the only silverware of his time as captain with a Scottish Cup final victory over Airdrieonians exactly six months later.

More than 600 competitive appearances – only Billy McNeill played more competitive games for the club – began to take their toll the following season. A chipped bone in his ankle, caused by kicks taken over a decade and a half when he rarely missed games, led surgeons to warn him that he faced developing a serious limp if he continued to play. In the statement to announce his retirement he drew comfort in the fact he would always be simply 'Paul McStay of Celtic and Scotland', his 76-cap haul making him the club's leading Scottish international.

Paul McStay factfile
Born: Hamilton, 22nd October 1964
Appearances: 677
Goals: 72
Full international appearances while at Celtic: 76 caps for Scotland
Honours:
League championship: 1985/86, 1987/88
Scottish Cup: 1985, 1988, 1989, 1995
League Cup: 1982/83

— GOLDIE OPPORTUNITY —

Third-choice Celtic goalkeeper Willie Goldie journeyed from scarf-clad supporter to first-teamer simply because he happened to be at the right bus stop on 1st October, 1960. Waiting for public transport to take him to the club's game at Airdrie, he was spotted from the team coach by chairman Bob Kelly, who dictated team selection. So impressed was Kelly by the keeper's commitment to the club, he instantly dropped regular No1 John Fallon and allowed Goldie to drop a few clangers in a two-goal defeat – his only game for the club.

— EUROPEAN NIGHTMARES —

The European defeats that still bring Celtic fans out in a cold sweat:

Neuchatel Xamax 5 Celtic 1, UEFA Cup second round, first leg, Switzerland, 22nd October 1991

From hubris to humiliation. Recently appointed manager Liam Brady thought so little of the Swiss opposition, he was confident of "winning the tie over there". Never mind that defensive injuries forced him to adopt an untried 3-5-2 formation. Roy Hodgson's men made merry with that system in wide areas to give Celtic their biggest beating in Europe at the time. Hossam Hassan, one of three Egyptians in home side's line-up, did most of the damage that couldn't be retrieved in the return leg, which Celtic won 1–0.

Artmedia Bratislava 5 Celtic 0, Champions League third qualifying round, first leg, 27th July 2005

It doesn't get any worse than this. The most excruciating Celtic managerial debut ever, some of the club's supporters wanted Gordon Strachan's first game in charge to be his last as the club suffered its heaviest defeat in 43 years of European football. Against supposed Slovakian makeweights appearing in continental competition for only a third time, Celtic plumbed unimaginable depths. The game started badly for the visitors when Chris Sutton sustained a fractured cheekbone in a collision with teammate Neil Lennon after only 17 minutes. Strachan's side only trailed 1–0 at half-time but, by continuing to chase an away goal, Celtic were shredded in the second half with Solvakian under-21 Juraj Halenar netting a hat-trick. "It is the worst night in football I've ever had," Strachan said afterwards. "I thought I'd been tested a lot as a player and a manager but this is a big one." To reach the Champions League group stage, Celtic were left with the task of becoming the first team to overturn a 5–0 deficit in Europe. Astonishingly, they almost did it with a brave 4–0 win at Celtic Park.

— METHUSELAH IN THE HOOPS . . . AND THE BHOY CHILD —

Even if modern training methods and a more scientific approach are allowing players to stay in the game longer, it is doubtful Celtic will ever field a performer older than the great Alec McNair. The full back was 41 years and four months when he turned out in his last game for the club – a 1–1 draw against Queen's Park at Celtic Park on 18th April 1925. His playing career was the longest ever at the club, having began in 1904.

Mark Fotheringham is believed to be the youngest player to turn out for Celtic. The midfielder was still five months from turning 17 when he made his debut in the league on 21st May 2000.

— CAN WE PLAY YOU EVERY WEEK? —

Celtic are unbeaten in all competitions against the following Scottish clubs:

	P	W	D	L	F	A
Livingston	19	18	1	0	57	3
Alloa Athletic	9	9	0	0	31	7
Montrose	9	8	1	0	40	6
East Stirling	8	8	0	0	26	5
Forfar Athletic	6	5	1	0	17	4
Stranraer	5	5	0	0	16	4
Brechin City	5	4	1	0	17	3
Berwick	4	4	0	0	16	0
Stenhousemuir	4	3	1	0	6	1
Gretna	3	3	0	0	8	1
Elgin City	2	2	0	0	9	1
Ross County	1	1	0	0	2	0

— KENNY GOES FOR YOUTH —

Celtic boss Kenny Dalglish surprised everyone by choosing youth team players Jim Goodwin, Ryan McCann and Brian McColligan for the home match against Dundee United on 21st May 2000. Despite a 2–0 win none of the trio ever played for the club again.

— OH SHOOT, IT'S PENALTIES —

Celtic have a decidedly mixed record in penalty shoot-outs in major competitions, having won only six of 13. Most notably, they were denied a third European Cup final appearance on penalties in 1972 and lost the first ever Scottish Cup final settled by this method in 1990.

Date	Competition	Result	Shoot-out score
19th April 1972	European Cup	Celtic 0 Inter 0	Lost 4–5
4th Sept 1985	League Cup	Hibs 4 Celtic 4	Lost 3–4
3rd Sept 1986	League Cup	Aberdeen 1 Celtic	Won 4–2
23rd Sept 1986	League Cup	Motherwell 2 Celtic 2	Won 5–4
30th Aug 1989	League Cup	Hearts 2 Celtic 2	Won 3–1
12th May 1990	Scottish Cup	Aberdeen 0 Celtic 0	Lost 8–9
3rd Sept 1991	League Cup	Airdrieonians 0 Celtic 0	Lost 2–4
27th Nov 1994	League Cup	Raith Rovers 2 Celtic 2	Lost 5–6
6th Dec 2001	UEFA Cup	Celtic 1 Valencia 0	Lost 4–5
6th Nov 2002	League Cup	Celtic 1 Partick Thistle 1	Won 5–4
7th Nov 2006	League Cup	Celtic 1 Falkirk 1	Lost 4–5
29th July 2007	Champs Lge	Celtic 1 Sp Moscow 1	Won 4–3
27th Jan 2009	League Cup	Dundee United	Won 11–10

— SEASONED-CELTS XI —

A team of players who signed for Celtic in their 30s (age and year of signing in brackets):

Alan Rough (36 – 1988); Paul Telfer (33 – 2005), Stefan Henchoz (31 – 2005), Pat Stanton (31 – 1976); Billy Stark (31– 1987), Roy Keane (34 – 2006), Paul Hartley (31– 2007), Lubo Moravcik (33 – 1998); *Frank McAvennie (33 –1992), Dion Dublin (36 – 2006), Wayne Biggins (32 – 1993)

* second spell

— FIRST IMPRESSIONS —

It takes seconds to make a good impression. In the case of Barry Robson, a mere 63 of them. That was all the time that elapsed between the midfielder arriving on the Pittodrie pitch as a 73rd minute substitute for Shunsuke Nakamura and netting with a free kick in a 5–1 win over Aberdeen on 10th February 2008. Signed from Dundee United for £1.1m nine days earlier, with his instant hit Robson become the very first Celtic player to score with his first touch in his first outing for the club.

Celtic striker Joe Craig can make such a claim in the international arena, however, the forward's headed goal against Sweden on 27th April 1977 coming only moments after he had replaced Kenny Burns.

— SPOT THE ODD ONES OUT —

Leaving aside the Co-operative Insurance Cup semi-final shoot-out in which all 11 players were required to step up, the club had seven different penalty-takers in 2008/09. There is no precedence in Celtic's history for such variety during a season. Perhaps it can be explained by the fact four of the eight spot-kicks Celtic were awarded were missed.

Date in season 2008/09

	Taker	Outcome		Competition Result
10th Aug	Barry Robson	Missed	League	Celtic 1 St Mirren 0
17th Sept	Barry Robson	Missed	Champ Lge	Celtic 0 Aalborg 0
20th Sept	Shaun Maloney	Missed	League	Kilmarnock 1 Celtic 3
23rd Sept	Georgios Samaras	Scored	League Cup	Celtic 4 Livingston 0
2nd Nov	Paul Hartley	Missed	League	Hearts 0 Celtic 2
16th Nov	Shunsuke Nakamura	Scored	League	Hamilton Accies 1 Celtic 2
28th Feb	Jan Vennegoor of Hesselink	Missed	League	Celtic 7 St Mirren 0
15th Mar	Aiden McGeady	Scored	League Cup final	Celtic 2 Rangers 0

— TAKING THE PEA —

The desperate insecurities Tony Cascarino laid bare in his ghosted autobiography were well hidden during an awful six-month stint at Celtic Park.

Despite scoring only four goals in 15 starts and 15 substitute appearances following a £1.1m move from Aston Villa in July 1991 that made him the club's first seven-figure signing, one – Cascarino – remained a joker around the club. Asked in a matchday programme profile what he would be if not a footballer, he replied: "a pea picker."

In February 1992, Cascarino headed to Stamford Bridge in a swap deal that brought Tom Boyd to Celtic. Happy to be rid of the under-performing Irish striker, the Celtic support immediately acclaimed Boyd with a chorus of "Let's all laugh at Chelsea".

— LITTLE GAIN IN SPAIN —

Celtic have played competitively on Spanish soil 13 times without recording a win:

Date	Competition	Result
26th Sept 1963	Fairs Cup	Valencia 4 Celtic 2
18th Nov 1965	Fairs Cup	Barcelona 3 Celtic 1
24th April 1974	European Cup	Atlético Madrid 2 Celtic 0
19th March 1980	European Cup	Real Madrid 3 Celtic 0
20th Oct 1982	European Cup	Real Sociedad 2 Celtic 0
18th Sept 1985	Cup Winners Cup	Atlético Madrid 1 Celtic 1
22nd Nov 2001	UEFA Cup	Valencia 1 Celtic 0
12th Dec 2002	UEFA Cup	Celta Vigo 2 Celtic 1
21st May 2003	UEFA Cup final*	Porto 3 Celtic 2
25th March 2004	UEFA Cup	Barcelona 0 Celtic 0
14th April 2004	UEFA Cup	Villarreal 2 Celtic 0
24th Nov 2004	Champs Lge	Barcelona 1 Celtic 1
4th March 2008	Champs Lge	Barcelona 2 Celtic 0
10th Dec 2008	Champs Lge	Villarreal 2 Celtic 0

*Match played in Seville

— THE LONE LOAN OLD FIRM PLAYER —

While a number of players have turned out for both Celtic and Rangers, goalkeeper Tom Sinclair is the only man to have played for one while his permanent employment was with the other.

When Celtic goalkeeper Davie Adams lacerated a palm in a pre-season Old Firm benefit match on 16th August 1906, Rangers immediately offered Sinclair till the wound healed. The loan signing proved a real hit, not conceding a goal in six consecutive league matches until finally being beaten on 29th September 1906. Sinclair's shut-outs record stood for almost a century.

— CELTIC LEGENDS: JIMMY McMENEMY —

Jimmy McMenemy: "The football pitch to him was like a chess board."

One of the finest inside forwards Scotland has produced, the wily Jimmy McMenemy more than lived up to his imposing nickname, 'Napoleon'.

In an 18-year Celtic career, McMenemy was a pivotal figure in two of the club's most lauded, and trophy-laden, sides. "The football pitch to him was like a chess board," manager Willie Maley said of his star player. "He was continually scheming and plotting and seldom, if ever, troubled himself with the physical side of the game – he had no need."

His name is often uttered as part of a rhyme of Celtic exaltation – Bennett, McMenemy, Quinn, Somers and Hamilton, a forward line that propelled the club to six straight championships in the 1900s and is claimed by some Celtic historians to have had no equal in world football at that time. McMenemy was the attacking orchestrator in this quintet. His full range of passing, burst of pace, precise heading and sublime craft that allowed him to dictate both tempo and direction of moves into enemy territory, made him an impossible player for opponents to shackle.

McMenemy signed for Celtic from local junior side Rutherglen Glencairn in 1902, having shown promise in trials. Then 22, he was a relative latecomer to senior football, having been forced to give up the game for two years when a spell working in a glass factory played havoc with his feet. Of slight build and with features not dissimilar to those of Napoleon, his feet remained nimble enough for him to still be an integral performer for Celtic in his late thirties.

The emergence of Patsy Gallacher saw McMenemy move to inside left in the early 1910s and both players were hugely influential in the Celtic side that claimed the first of four consecutive titles in 1914. By then McMenemy had earned 11 Scotland caps without ever being on the losing side, making particularly memorable contributions to victories over England in 1910 and 1914. He also represented the Scottish League and after one wartime game against England received the following tribute from teammate Adam Scott Duncan: "I don't think I ever played a better game. Anyone could play with McMenemy. He's one of the few to whom the term genius has been applied without hysterics."

Although there was no Scottish Cup during the First World War – during which McMenemy combined playing with working in a munitions factory – he stands alongside Billy McNeill and Bobby Lennox as the only Celts with seven winners' medals in the competition. His last triumph wasn't with the club but as a 40-year-old member of the Partick Thistle side who defeated Rangers in 1921. Quite an achievement considering he had retired three years earlier, only to return and inspire Celtic to the championship in 1918/19, his 10th such honour.

McMenemy later returned to Celtic as a coach, and he played a huge role in two titles success as Willie Maley's assistant from 1935 to 1940. His son John later played for Celtic and his other sons, Harry and Frank, also enjoyed senior careers that peaked with Newcastle United and Hamilton respectively. Former Southampton manager Lawrie McMenemy is his great-nephew.

Jimmy McMenemy factfile
Born: Rutherglen, 23rd August 1880
Died: Robroyston, 23rd June 1965
Appearances: 515
Goals: 168
Full international appearances while at Celtic: 12 caps for Scotland
Honours:
League championship: 1904/05, 1905/06, 1906/07, 1907/08, 1908/09, 1909/10, 1913/14, 1914/15, 1915/16, 1916/17, 1918/19
Scottish Cup: 1904, 1907, 1908, 1911, 1912, 1914

— THE STAND-OUT SHOOT-OUT —

It wasn't so much the mother and father of penalty shoot-outs that was played out at Hampden on 27th January 2009 but the grandmother and grandfather of them. With their Co-operative Insurance Cup semi-final scoreless after 120 minutes, Celtic and Dundee United served up the longest spot-kick decider in the history of the Scottish game.

It lasted all of 25 kicks. Artur Boruc became the first keeper to take a penalty competitively for the club since Frank Haffey 46 years earlier. Haffey missed in normal play, however, while Boruc sent a curling effort high into the net with such aplomb supporters mischievously voted it their goal of the season.

The outrageous drama concluded when Scott McDonald converted to make him the only player with a Scottish club to have scored two penalties in the same shoot-out. It was a miss from Wilo Flood, who had netted his initial penalty, that allowed the Australian to settle the issue. It was Flood's last act as a United player. Two days later he joined Celtic.

CELTIC
Home and Away Kits
1888-2010

www.historicalkits.co.uk

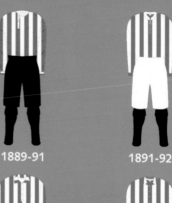
1888-89

1889-91

1891-92

1893-95

1895-97

1897-98

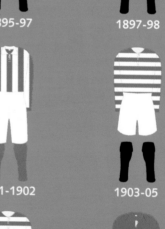

1898-99

1901-1902

1903-05

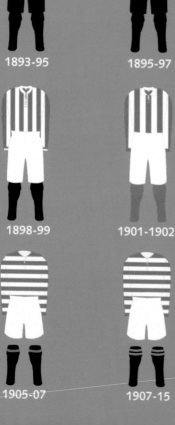

1905-07

1907-15

1910-18 (change)

1913-19

1918-19 (change)

1919-20 (change)

1919-21

1921-22 (change)

1921-22
(late season change)

1923-24 (change)

1924-25 (change)

1924-26

1925-26 (change)

1926-27 (change)

1926-27

1926-27 (change)

1927-28

1927-28 (change)

1927-28 (change)

1928-1930

1928-29 (change)

1929-30 (change)

1930-31

1930-31 (change)

1931-32

1931-33 (change)

April 1931 (change)

1932-36

late 1932

1934-35 (change)

1935-36 (change)

1936-56

1948-49 (change)

1955-1958 (change)

1956-1960

1958-60 (change)

1960-62

1960-65 (change)

1960-65 (third)

1963-65

1963 (March-May)

1964-66 (change)

1965-72

1966-67 (change)

1967-68 (change)

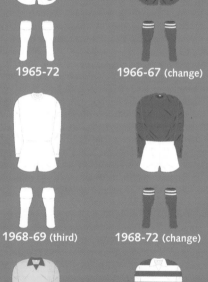

1968-69 (third)

1968-72 (change)

1970-71 (change)

1972-73 (change)

1972-76

1973-77 (change)

1976-77

1977-80

1977-80 (change)

1977-78 (third)

1980-82

1982-84

1982-83 (change)

1983-84 (change)

**1983-84
(European change)**

1984-86

1984-85 (change)

1984-85 (third)

1986-87

1986-87 (change)

1986-87 (third)

1987-89

1987-88 (change)

1989-91

1989-91 (change)

1991-92

1991-92 (change)

1991-92 (third)

1992-1993

1992-3 (change)

1993-95

1994-95 (change)

1994-96 (third)

1995-97

1996-97 (change)

1997-99

1997-98 (change)

1998-99 (change)

1999-2001

1999-2000
(change)

2000-01 (change)

2001-02

2001-02 (change)

2001-02 (third)

2002-04

2002-03 (third)

2003-04 (change)

2004-05

2004-05 (change)

2005-07

2005-06 (change)

2005-07 (third)

2006-07 (change)

2006-08 (third)

1993-95

1994-95 (change)

1994-96 (third)

1995-97

1996-97 (change)

1997-99

1997-98 (change)

1998-99 (change)

1999-2001

1999-2000
(change)

2000-01 (change)

2001-02

2001-02 (change)

2001-02 (third)

2002-04

2002-03 (third)

2003-04 (change)

2004-05

2004-05 (change)

2005-07

2005-06 (change)

2005-07 (third)

2006-07 (change)

2006-08 (third)

2007-08

2007-08 (change)

2008-09

2008-10

2009-10 (change)

— OUT OF INDIA —

Mohammed Abdul Salim's brief spell with Celtic in the 1930s might be termed a 'footnote' in Celtic's history – incredibly, he played with his bare feet strapped in bandages.

Born in Calcutta, after helping the Mohammedan Sporting Club to five consecutive Indian titles his cousin encouraged him to try his luck in Europe. And so it was that in 1937, at the age of at 23, he arrived in London on ocean liner The City of Cairo. Finding the capital unappealing, he looked to Glasgow, second city of the Empire, and was given a trial by Celtic manager Willie Maley. He impressed enough to win a contract and so become the first player from the sub-continent to sign for a European football club.

Salim didn't actually make any competitive appearances for Celtic but sported his unusual footwear for friendly wins against Hamilton, beaten 5–1, and Galston, thrashed 7–1. Inevitably, the exotic forward grabbed more than his share of coverage in the local press. After the Galston match, under a headline which read 'Indian Juggler – New Style', The Scottish Daily Express reported: "Ten twinkling toes of Salim, Celtic FC's player from India hypnotised the crowd at Parkhead. He balances the ball on his big toe, lets it run down the scale to his little toe, twirls it and hops on one foot around the defender."

Soon, though, Salim was hopping back to India. Homesickness got the better of him and although Celtic attempted to encourage him to stay by offering him five per cent of the takings from a charity match in his honour, he declined the offer. Instead he asked that the money, said to be a somewhat unbelievable £1,800, be given to an orphan charity to which the club made yearly donations.

When he fell ill in later life – he died in 1980 – it is said that his son Rashid wrote to the club under the guise of asking for financial assistance, but really to see if the club remembered his father. Salim died before a reply came with the offer of "all sorts of reassuring help" and a cheque for £100.

— UNFORGETTABLE GAMES:
FOR QUEEN AND CELTIC —

Celtic 2 Hibernian 0, Coronation Cup Final, Hampden, 20th May 1953

Celtic supporters revel in the Coronation Cup success. It appeals to their prejudices. Rightly, they see a delicious irony in a competition organised to celebrate the coronation of Queen Elizabeth II being won by their team. After all, this is a club whose followers, in harbouring Irish republican sympathies rooted in their origins, have the greatest contempt for the monarchy of any British side.

It also tickles them that they had no right to be asked to take part in the tournament. It was supposed to be an eight-team knock-out event contested by the leading sides from either side of the border. On merit, Arsenal, Manchester United, Tottenham Hotspur and Newcastle United, joined Scottish teams Rangers, Hibernian and Aberdeen. Celtic, with only one trophy success since the league title of 1938, were invited to swell the gate receipts. They did so much more.

After being drawn against English league champions Arsenal, Celtic were expected to enjoy no more than one big payday. But galvanised by the recruitment of new signing Neil Mochan from Middlesbrough, a goal scored directly from a corner kick by Bobby Collins capped a stirring performance before strikes from Mochan and Bertie Peacock put paid to Manchester United in the semi-final, both games staged at Hampden.

So Hibs, victors over Spurs and Newcastle, were left standing in their path. Hampden, for an occasion honouring Queen and country, was treated to the spectacle of two 'Irish' clubs bathing it in green-and-white in front of a massive crowd of 117,060. The attendance would have been even greater but for the gates being shut amid fears of overcrowding.

Once again, it was Mochan who put Celtic ahead, this time with a 30-yard piledriver in the 28th minute. The goal was against the run of play, however, and Hibs continued to threaten through their 'Famous Five' forward line. Yet, despite numerous chances, they couldn't get past the magnificent John Bonnar in the Celtic goal. Then, with three minutes left, Celtic clinched the cup when Jimmy Walsh netted after a rare breakaway.

There was no doubt about the man of the match, though. One report described Bonnar's performance as "bordering on the miraculous" and afterwards thousands gathered at the front entrance of Hampden to chant his name.

Celtic: Bonnar, Haughey, Rollo, Evans, Stein, McPhail, Collins, Walsh, Mochan, Peacock, Fernie

Hibernian: Younger, Govan, Paterson, Buchanan, Howie, Combe, Smith, Johnstone, Reilly, Turnbull, Ormond

— CELTIC CAPTAINS —

Celtic's longest-serving captain is Billy McNeill, who held the post for 12 years. The full roll-call, which includes both club captains and acting team captains is:

1888–97	James Kelly
1897–99	Dan Doyle
1899–1903	Sandy McMahon
1903–06	Willie Orr
1906–11	James Hay
1911–17	'Sunny Jim' Young
1917–20	Alec McNair
1920–23	William Cringan
1923–25	Charlie Shaw
1925–29	Willie McStay
1929–34	Jimmy McStay
1934–35	Peter McGonagle
1935-40	Willie Lyon
1940-48	Bobby Hogg
1948–52	John McPhail
1952–53	Sean Fallon
1953–55	Jock Stein
1955–56	Jock Stein/Bobby Evans
1955–57	Bobby Evans
1957–61	Bertie Peacock
1961–63	Duncan MacKay
1963–75	Billy McNeill
1975–77	Kenny Dalglish

1977–87	Danny McGrain
1987–90	Roy Aitken
1990–97	Paul McStay
1997–2002	Tom Boyd
2002–04	Paul Lambert
2004–05	Jackie McNamara
2005–07	Neil Lennon
2007–	Stephen McManus

— 'LIZZIE' LAMPOONED IN SONG —

The relish with which the Celtic faithful celebrated the 1953 Coronation Cup victory was reflected in the composition of a mocking ditty to denote the occasion. It remained a favourite of Celtic social gatherings for many years.

Said Lizzie To Philip: The Coronation Cup Song

Said Lizzie to Philip as they sat down to dine,
"I've just had a note from an old friend of mine,
"His name is Big Geordie, he's loyal and true,
"And his nose is my favourite colour of blue.

"He says that the Rangers are right on their game,
"And asks for a trophy to add to their fame
"I'll send up a trophy the Rangers can win".
Said Philip to Lizzie, "Watch the Celts don't step in."

Said Lizzie to Philip, "They don't stand a chance,
"I'll send up my Gunners to lead them a dance,
"With the Celtic defeated the way will be clear,
"For a cup for the Rangers in my crowning year."

But oh what a blow to the old boys in blue,
The Celts beat the Arsenal and Manchester too,
Beat the Hibs in the final and lo and behold,
All Hampden was covered in green, white and gold.

Said Lizzie to Philip when she heard the news,
"A blow has been struck to my loyal True Blues,
"Oh tell me dear Philip, for I ought to know,
"How to beat Glasgow Celtic and keep them below."

Said Philip to Lizzie, "There's only one way,
"And that's been no secret for many a day,
"To beat Glasgow Celtic you'll have to deport,
"The whole Fenian army that gives them support!"

— THE FINALS FIRMLY REMEMBERED —

Domestic cup finals in which Celtic and Rangers face each other down tend to be set apart from others in the eyes of the two clubs' supporters.

Honours are even in the 15 Scottish Cup Finals the clubs have played in the competition, with seven wins apiece and the cup not awarded on the other occasion. Celtic's record in the League Cup Final against their bitter rivals is horrendous, however. They have only won four out of 12, and just one in the past eight.

Scottish Cup

Date	Result
17th Feb 1894	Rangers 3 Celtic 1
22nd April 1899	Celtic 2 Rangers 0
16th April 1904	Celtic 3 Rangers 2
10th April 1909	Celtic 2 Rangers 2
17th April 1909 (replay)	Celtic 1 Rangers 1*
6th April 1928	Rangers 4 Celtic 0
4th May 1963	Rangers 1 Celtic 1
15th May 1963 (replay)	Rangers 3 Celtic 0
23rd April 1966	Rangers 0 Celtic 0
27th April 1966 (replay)	Rangers 1 Celtic 0
26th April 1969	Celtic 4 Rangers 0
8th May 1971	Celtic 1 Rangers 1
12th May 1971 (replay)	Celtic 2 Rangers 1
5th May 1973	Rangers 3 Celtic 2
7th May 1977	Celtic 1 Rangers 0
10th May 1980	Celtic 1 Rangers 0 (aet)
20th May 1989	Celtic 1 Rangers 0
29th May 1999	Rangers 1 Celtic 0
4th May 2002	Rangers 3 Celtic 2

*The SFA withheld the cup in 1909 after a riot following the replay.

League Cup

Date	Result
19th Oct 1957	Celtic 7 Rangers 1
24th Oct 1964	Rangers 2 Celtic 1
23rd Oct 1965	Celtic 2 Rangers 1
29th Oct 1966	Celtic 1 Rangers 0
24th Oct 1970	Rangers 1 Celtic 0
25th Oct 1975	Rangers 1 Celtic 0
18th March 1978	Rangers 2 Celtic 1 (aet)
4th Dec 1982	Celtic 2 Rangers 1
25th March 1984	Rangers 3 Celtic 2 (aet)
26th Oct 1986	Rangers 2 Celtic 1
28th Oct 1990	Rangers 2 Celtic 1
16th March 2003	Rangers 2 Celtic 1
15th March 2009	Celtic 2 Rangers 0 (aet)

— FROM DOMINATION TO DIMINISHMENT —

Between 1965/66 and 1969/70, Celtic owned the League Cup. Their five straight wins is the longest victorious period of any club in the 61 seasons of the competition.

They then appeared in the next eight finals, creating a world record of 13 consecutive final appearances in a national cup. But they won only one of these, in 1974/75. Between their 1969/70 and 1997/98 successes they lifted the trophy on only two occasions in 27 seasons.

— STEIN STAYS AT HOME —

Jock Stein officially never signed an overseas outfield player while Celtic manager, a period spanning from 1965 to 1978. Iceland forward Johannes Edvaldsson joined in August 1975 but assistant Sean Fallon was then in charge as Stein recovered from injuries sustained in a serious car crash a month earlier. It is generally believed Stein put the move in progress before his accident, however. Danish goalkeeper Bent Martin, signed in January 1966 after a trial period, is the only foreign signing Stein completed the paperwork on.

— KELLY COUNTS FOR GOOD AND BAD —

Nearly 40 years a director and 23 years as chairman, Bob Kelly's contribution to Celtic laid bare the best and worst aspects of the club being run as a fiefdom by the Kelly and White families for almost a century. In part, indeed, his reputation is besmirched by his family associations with nephews Kevin and Michael, members of the board who took the club to the brink of receivership before Fergus McCann's takeover in 1994 ended the destructive dynastical control.

But that is not the central reason for the ambivalence towards him. As Celtic history *The Glory and the Dream* put it of Kelly: ". . . he was the ultimate authority . . . very few decisions, no matter how small, were made without his prior knowledge or approval. Autocratic in manner and severe in appearance, he was a benevolent despot exercising strict control with the best interest of the club, as he saw them, at heart, and like most despots, imbued with a philosophy that was conservative and traditional."

Dubbed 'Mr Celtic' by the press, Kelly was the son of Celtic's first captain James Kelly. In 1931 he became a director on the death of his father, latterly the club's chairman. He assumed that same honour in 1947 and presided over a desperate post-war period. He was a backward-thinking figure. But in a laudable, if impractical, sense. He believed in football played in the most sporting manner by home-grown products from whom the highest standards of behaviour and discipline were obligatory and whose fates, on and off the field, were strictly in his domain.

Baffling team selections considered to have cost Celtic Scottish Cup final success against Clyde (1955), Hearts (1956), Dunfermline (1961) and Rangers (1963) are attributed to his imposing line-ups on the hopelessly undermined manager Jimmy McGrory. Bertie Auld and Paddy Crerand were infamously sold because they were temperamental and would not meekly tolerate his meddling.

Kelly is still championed, though, for his passionate and articulate defence of the club's right to fly the Irish tricolour in 1952. Bizarrely, the game's legislators decreed this had the potential to incite crowd trouble in the wake of serious hooliganism at the Old Firm New Year's Day derby.

But Kelly's determination to preserve tradition in all forms proved severely damaging to the club's football prospects. Although he is given credit for the appointment of Jock Stein in 1965, by then he had no choice. He had allowed the club to slide towards oblivion in the early 1960s because, he claimed later, he believed supporters would be resistant to a manager who was not Catholic, which, in fairness to him, he had never made a necessity for the role as club captain. He initially tried to employ Stein as assistant to Sean Fallon and then joint manager with the Irishman. His reluctance to appoint Stein as the master of all he surveyed, the only condition on which an offer would be accepted, probably owed as much to him hating the thought of losing his day-to-day involvement in the running of the team.

Perhaps what best sums him up is how he reacted to Celtic becoming the first British club to reach the European Cup final, which was, of course, won in 1967. Stein delivered that momentous achievement by going completely against the grain and securing a niggardly 0–0 draw in the second leg of the semi-final away to Dukla Prague. As the Celtic players celebrated in the dressing room, legend has it Kelly burst in and, believing the suffocating tactics to be an affront to 'the Celtic way', told Stein that he must "never play that way again".

— A THUMPING IN ANYONE'S LANGUAGE —

Celtic's 6–0 drubbing of Aberdeen at Pittodrie on 11th December 1999 is the only competitive game in Britain in which a team has had scorers of six different nationalities. The men to find the net for Celtic that afternoon were: Paul Lambert (Scotland, 21 mins), Stephane Mahe (France, 28 mins), Lubo Moravcík (Slovakia, 67 mins), Mark Viduka (Australia, 75 mins), Regi Blinker (Holland, 81 mins) and Ian Wright (England, 87 mins).

— McGRORY SCORES . . . HAMDPEN ROARS —

Jimmy McGrory is credited with sparking the 'Hampden Roar'. The sustained, structure-shaking shouting in international games with which Scotland's national stadium became synonymous was first generated by the 134,170 fans who saw the Celtic striker score a late winner to complete a double in Scotland's 2–1 victory over England on 1st April 1931.

— LEADING MARKSMEN —

With a phenomenal record of 468 goals for the club, inter-war striker Jimmy McGory is easily Celtic's leading goalscorer. Here's the top ten for all competitions, and just for league football:

Top ten all-time goalscorers (all competitions)

1.	Jimmy McGrory (1921–37)	468
2.	Bobby Lennox (1961–80)	273
3.	Henrik Larsson (1997–2004)	242
4.	Stevie Chalmers (1959–71)	219
5.	Jimmy Quinn (1901–15)	217
6.	Patsy Gallacher (1911–26)	192
7.	John Hughes (1959–71)	188
8.	Sandy McMahon (1890–1903)	177
9.	Jimmy McMenemy (1902–20)	168
10.	Kenny Dalglish (1967–77)	167

Top ten all-time league goalscorers

1.	Jimmy McGrory (1921–37)	395
2.	Jimmy Quinn (1901–15)	187
3.	Patsy Gallacher (1911–26)	186
4.	Henrik Larsson (1997–2004)	174
5.	Bobby Lennox (1961–80)	167
6.	Stevie Chalmers (1959–71)	147
7.	Jimmy McMenemy (1902–20)	144
8.	Sandy McMahon (1890–1903)	130
9.	Adam McLean (1917–28)	128
10.	Jimmy McColl (1913–20)	117

— THE SUB HAT-TRICK —

Andy Payton is the only player to score a hat-trick for Celtic as a substitute. He achieved this feat in a 9–1 win away to Arboath in a third round League Cup tie on 25th August 1993, after coming on for the injured Charlie Nicholas with half an hour gone.

Frank McAvennie also netted a triple that night to earn the man of the match award. In recognition, he was presented with a box of Arbroath smokies by the hosts.

— A GRAND OLD TEAM TO MANAGE . . .
FOR SOME —

In 130 years, Celtic have had just 15 managers, with one acting
manager and one caretaker manager. In the club's first 104 years,
only six men held the position on a permanent basis, a committee
picking the team during the first nine years.

Manager	Major honours
Willie Maley (1987–40)	16 championships, 14 Scottish Cups, Glasgow Exhibition Trophy (1902), Empire Exhibition Trophy (1938)
Jimmy McStay (1940–45)	—
Jimmy McGrory (1945–65)	1 championship, 2 Scottish Cups, 2 League Cups, St Mungo Cup (1951), Coronation Cup (1953)
Jock Stein* (1965–78)	10 championships, 8 Scottish Cups, 6 League Cups, European Cup (1967)
Billy McNeill (1978–83)	3 championships, 1 Scottish Cup, 1 League Cup
Davie Hay (1983–87)	1 championship, 1 Scottish Cup
Billy McNeill (1987–91)	1 championship, 2 Scottish Cups
Liam Brady (1991–93)	—
Lou Macari (1993–94)	—
Tommy Burns (1994–97)	1 Scottish Cup
Wim Jansen (1997–98)	1 championship, 1 Scottish Cup
Jozef Vengloš (1998–99)	—
John Barnes (1999–2000)	—
Kenny Dalglish (2000)**	1 League Cup
Martin O'Neill (2000–05)	3 championships, 3 Scottish Cups, 1 League Cup
Gordon Strachan (2005–2009)	3 championships, 1 Scottish Cup, 2 League Cups

*Sean Fallon was acting manager for season 1975/76 while Stein
was convalescing after a car crash. No honours were won.
**Dalglish, who arrived as director of football and half of a
'dream team' with John Barnes, was made caretaker manager
when the former English international was sacked.

— A GRAND OLD TUNE . . . OR TWO —

It's cheesy in the extreme. Yet matchdays at Celtic Park wouldn't be the same without the tannoy system crackling to the whiny voice of late Glasgow entertainer Glen Daly belting out *The Celtic Song*.

- The opening line "Sure it's a grand old team to play for" has in itself become the stuff of legend, headline and book title fame. Daly, accompanied on jaunty accordion by Will Starr Jr, recorded the self-penned club anthem in 1961. Lyrics are credited to 'Liam Mallory', believed to be an alias for Daly. It may well have had its origins in a similar song that was popular with Belfast Celtic for many years prior to the Daly recording. Another story runs that it was penned by Mick McLaughlin, 'Garngad Mick' who is alleged to have written the Celtic ditty *Hampden in the Sun*. He is said to have sold Daly the lyrics for a fiver. *The Celtic Song* is believed to have gone on to achieve worldwide sales of one million.

- When he took over the club in 1994, Fergus McCann believed Daly's recording was cringeworthy and outdated and he floated the idea of commissioning a new version. After being encouraged to recognise he was missing the point about a club tradition, the plan was dropped.

- In the 1970s Don Revie was keen for the song to be adapted and played at England games. A version now fills the air at Goodison before Everton games and Aberdeen supporters have their own take on it.

- The success of *The Celtic Song* for Pye Records led them to ask Daly to record *The Rangers Song* as a follow-up. Lifelong Celtic fan Daly declined and he, as *A Celtic A–Z* puts it, "had to educate the English-based company's executives about the nature of Glasgow's football rivalry". The message didn't quite get through as the late Buddy Logan recorded a Rangers version. It didn't catch on.

- Celtic supporters do not sing Daly's version but a hybrid of that and *Hail Hail*, an early 1960s terracing chant that used as its source the military marching song *Hail, Hail, the Gang's All Here* (with the next line "What the deuce do we care?"). Written by DA Estron, it was based on *With Cat-like Tread* from the

Gilbert and Sullivan comic opera *The Pirates of Penzance* – a song which, in turn, leant heavily on the Anvil chorus from Verdi's 1853 opera *Il Trovatore*. Just to confuse matters thoroughly, Daly also recorded another original song, *Hail Hail Celtic*, based on the *Hail Hail* terracing chant. Only the intro survives in the supporters' version of *Hail Hail/Grand Old Team*.

The Celtic Song (original that is played over the tannoy)

Sure it's a grand old team to play for,
Sure it's a grand old team to bedad,
And when you read its history,
It's enough to make your heart go sad,
God bless them.
We don't care what if we win, lose or draw
Darn the hair we care,
For we only know that there's going to be a show,
And the Glasgow Celtic will be there.

Sure it's the best darn team in Scotland,
And the players all are grand,
We support the Celtic,
As they are the finest in the land,
We love them.
We'll be there to give the Bhoys a cheer
When the league flag flies,
And it cheers us up when we know the Scottish Cup
Is coming home to rest at Paradise.

Sure it's a grand old team to play for,
Sure it's a grand old team bedad,
And when you read its history,
It's enough to make your heart go sad,
God bless them.
We don't care if we win lose or draw,
Darn the hair do we care,
For we only know that there's going to be a show,
And the Glasgow Celtic will be there,
And the Glasgow Celtic will be there.

Hail Hail/Grand Old Team (as sung by Celtic supporters)

Hail Hail, the Celts are here,
What the hell do we care,
What the hell do we care,
Hail Hail, the Celts are here,
What the hell do we care now?

For it's a grand old team to play for,
For it's a grand old team to see,
And if you know your history,
Its enough to make your heart
Go oh-oh-oh!

We don't care what the animals say,
What the hell do we care,
For we only know,
That there's gonna be a show,
And the Glasgow Celtic will be there.

Sure it's the best darn team in Scotland
and the players they are grand,
We support the Celtic
'Cause they are the finest in the land we love them.
We'll be there to give the Bhoys a cheer
When the league flag flies,
And the cheers go up 'cause we know the Scottish Cup
Is coming home to rest at Paradise.

— A HAT-TRICK OF HAT-TRICKS —

In 1984 three different Celtic players scored hat tricks in consecutive matches:

Date	Player	Result
17th Nov 1984	Brian McClair	Hearts 1 Celtic 5
24th Nov 1984	Frank McGarvey	Celtic 7 St Mirren 1
11th Dec 1984	Maurice Johnston	Celtic 5 Dundee 1

— MESSIAH MARTIN —

Martin O'Neill: an inspiration

It is said that for a first meeting with their new manager on the opening day of pre-season in July 2000, the Celtic players were told to gather in the dressing room at the club's stadium. Legend has it that Martin O'Neill burst through the door, drew them daggers as he scanned the room, then raged: "21 points? 21 f****** points? It won't be happening again." Before turning heel and storming out.

It didn't happen again. The 21-point record title winning margin for Dick Advocaat's Rangers, achieved against the ill-conceived 'dream team' of John Barnes and Kenny Dalglish, was overturned in extraordinary fashion. O'Neill effected a 36-point swing to blitz the title – on the way to guiding the club to a first treble in 32 years.

As one of the hottest tickets in the Premiership after top half of the table finishes and double League Cup success with unfancied Leicester City, O'Neill was supposed to be out of reach for Celtic. But the former Nottingham Forest midfielder accepted the onerous challenge. On doing so, the charismatic Irishman said his late father had once told him to "walk all the way to Glasgow" if he ever had the chance to become Celtic manager.

In five years at Celtic, O'Neill won three titles, three Scottish Cups and one League Cup, and might easily have claimed more silverware. Two championships were lost to Alex McLeish's Rangers on the last day, in 2003 and 2005. The latter came when O'Neill's impassioned focus had been understandably diluted by tending for his cancer-stricken wife Geraldine. He then ended his "love affair" with the club by taking a sabbatical from the game so he could be by her side as she received treatment for lymphoma.

The two-goal difference deficit that condemned Celtic to a barren season of 2003 is forgiven because that season he led the club to a first European final in 33 years. Indeed, that UEFA Cup run to the Seville showpiece, lost to José Mourinho's soon-to-be-Champions League winners Porto after extra time, served up thrilling wins away to Liverpool and Blackburn that gave the lie to O'Neill's side being a purely functional outfit. A host of other European nights in Glasgow, which saw Juventus, Porto, Barcelona and Lyon shaken by the drive and commitment with which O'Neill had imbued his charges, also proved that there was more to his side than mere pragmatism.

He sought physical presence and power from his Celtic teams, but they could play too. Certainly their passing game was direct and efficient and designed to see the ball moved up front as quickly as possible. But that was an understandable approach since he was fortunate to be bequeathed the club's greatest matchwinner of the post-Lisbon Lions era in Henrik Larsson. Making the most of this good luck, the Irishman proved himself the most astute manager at the club since Jock Stein by surrounding the Swede with teammates chosen to give the striker the best possible platform for his wondrous scoring talents.

O'Neill got so much right, so quickly. And though much is made of the fact he was given £16m to splurge on players immediately, in recruiting Chris Sutton, Joos Valgaeren, Alan Thompson, Neil Lennon, and Didier Agathe for £35,000, he established a core – along with £6m John Hartson and free transfer Bobo Baldé a year later – that sustained Celtic until age caught up with them in the post-Larsson season of 2004/05. In his first four years at Celtic, O'Neill, by turns witty, charming, sarcastic, stubborn and always engaging, proved the inspiration for as many title wins and European victories as the club had recorded in the previous 18 years. That is how he will be remembered.

— JUNGLE FEVER —

As Liverpool had the Kop, so Celtic had the Jungle. The covered terracing on the Janefield Street side of the ground disappeared when the old Celtic Park made way for a new 60,000 all-seater stadium in 1994. It is still mourned. And has been since it effectively passed into history the previous summer. Then, the old board's every-cost-spared approach to bringing the ground into line with the recommendations of the Taylor report meant bolting seats on to the Jungle slopes to create a 'stand'. It was never that. The frisson created by the swaying, rocking mass of fans in the covered enclosure was all down to them being crammed together, shoulder-to-shoulder, to become an amorphous body.

The Jungle served as the Greek chorus for the club's faithful. It was their political wing, home for the hard – often unreconstructed, and certainly Irish republican and anti-establishment – core. The club's supporting soul, it could be a dark place. The banana throwing at Rangers' Mark Walters in 1988, or the gleeful chants composed for every IRA bombing or assassination through the 1970s and 1980s, were testimony to that.

Visiting players were often said to be frightened of straying too close to the Jungle because of the wildness of those within it. Hence one explanation, the most obvious, for the name.

Another theory is put forward in *A Celtic A-Z*, which suggests the nickname came into vogue just after the Second World War. Then the enclosure was an uncovered, crumbling, ash-covered terracing. It is suggested that servicemen returning from the undergrowths of the Far East might have jokingly referred to their spectating conditions as no better than those jungle battlegrounds.

— TONY'S HUDDLE —

Now that Tony Mowbray is Celtic manager, it adds piquancy to the fact he is the man responsible for the famous Celtic huddle, the pre-match ritual which sees the players form a circle, link arms, lean into one another and exchange words of encouragement to gee themselves up in the seconds leading up to kick-off.

As the club prepared to return to a partially rebuilt Celtic Park in the summer of 1995 following a desperate league season at Hampden, centre back Mowbray wanted a show of unity from the players with which the supporters could identify, and to which they would respond. He hit upon the idea of the huddle, a feature of American sporting occasions that he had spotted watching ice hockey. It became a part of Celtic's on-field preparations during a pre-season tour of Germany that year, and is now firmly classified as a beloved tradition.

Dog gone it, the practice has even provided the look and name of Celtic's matchday mascot, one Hoopy the Huddle Hound.

— THE INTERNATIONALS —

Obviously, Celtic have had dozens of Scottish internationals on their books. But many other nations, in the guise of current or former full internationals, have been represented among those who have donned the club's colours competitively. Here's the full list:

Country	Players (Celtic careers)
Albania	Rudi Vata (1992–96)
Australia	Mark Viduka (1998–2000),
	Scott McDonald (2007–now)
Brazil	Rafael Scheidt (1999–2000),
	Juninho (2004–05)
Belgium	Joos Valgaeren (2000–05)
Bulgaria	Stilian Petrov (1998–2005)
Cameroon	Jean-Joël Perrier Doumbé (2007-2009)
China	Du Wei (2006)
Czechoslovakia	Lubo Moravcík (1998–2002)
Czech Republic	Jirí Jarošík (2006–08)
Canada	Joe Kennaway (1931–40)
Denmark	Morten Wieghorst (1995–2002),
	Marc Rieper (1997–98),
	Thomas Gravesen (2006–2008)
East Germany	Andreas Thom (1995–98)
England	Ian Wright (1999–2000),
	Chris Sutton (2000–05),
	Alan Thompson (2000–07),
	Steve Guppy (2001–04),
	Michael Gray (2003),
	Dion Dublin (2006)
Germany	Andreas Thom (1995–98),
	Andreas Hinkel (2008–now)
Greece	Georgios Samaras (2008)
Guinea	Bobo Baldé (2001–2009),
	Momo Sylla (2001–05),
	Mo Camara (2005–06)
Holland	Pierre van Hooijdonk (1995–97),
	Jan Vennegoor of Hesselink (2006–2009)
Iceland	Jóhannes Eðvaldsson (1975–80),
	Teddy Bjarnason (2004–08)

THE CELTIC MISCELLANY

Ireland	Patsy Gallacher (1911–26)
Irish Free State	Peter Kavanagh (1929–32)
Israel	Eyal Berkovic (1999–2000)
Ivory Coast	Olivier Tébily (1999–2002)
Jamaica	Gil Heron (1951–52)
Japan	Shunsuke Nakamura (2005–2009)
New Zealand	Chris Killen (2007–now)
Norway	Harald Brattbakk (1997–2000), Vidar Riseth (1998–2001)
Northern Ireland	Peter Kavanagh (1929–32), Charlie Tully (1948–59), Bertie Peacock (1949–61), Anton Rogan (1986–91), Allen McKnight (1986–88), Neil Lennon (2000–07)
Poland	Dariusz Dziekanowski (1989–92), Dariusz Wdowczyk (1989–94), Maciej Żurawski (2005–07), Artur Boruc (2005–now)
Portugal	Jorge Cadete (1995–97)
Republic of Ireland	Sean Fallon (1950–58), Charlie Gallagher (1958–70), Paddy Turner (1963–64), Joe Haverty (1964), Pat Bonner (1978–94), Chris Morris (1987–92), Mick McCarthy (1987–89), Tommy Coyne (1989–93), Tony Cascarino (1991–92), Liam Miller (1997–2004), Colin Healy (1998–2003), Aiden McGeady (2004–now), Roy Keane (2006)
Senegal	Henri Camara (2004–05)
Slovakia	Lubo Moravčík (1998–2002), Stanislav Varga (2003–06)
Sweden	Henrik Larsson (1997–2004), Johan Mjällby (1998–2004), Magnus Hedman (2002–05)

Switzerland	Ramon Vega (2000–01),
	Stéphane Henchoz (2005)
Venuezula	Fernando de Ornellas (2000)
Wales	John Hartson (2001–06),
	Craig Bellamy (2005)

— NUMBERS UP —

For years Celtic would not countenance 'disrupting' their famous hoops by putting numbers on the back. They got round the problem by having numbers on their shorts, these first appearing in a friendly against Sparta Rotterdam on 14th May 1960.

By the mid-1970s UEFA rules made it compulsory for Celtic to wear number patches for European games. Scotland came into line with this regulation for the start of the 1994/95 season, new owner Fergus McCann's first in charge. McCann strongly felt that this requirement was unnecessary in the domestic environment. He even considered paying a fine for every game Celtic went without strip numbers until eventually deciding to relent.

— DUFF BY NAME . . . —

The open-to-all nature of Celtic's recruitment policy from the club's early days perhaps finds its best expression in early goalkeeper Tom Duff. Unabashed Catholic club or not, Celtic had no qualms about the Ayrshire gent becoming the first Orangeman to play for them and signed him in 1891, turning to him in nine first-class matches.

The only problem seems to have been that he proved Duff by name and by nature come New Year's Day 1892. On an afternoon when Celtic first used nets he was forced to pick the ball out of his 11 times – on three occasions after disallowed goals – in an 8–0 friendly defeat against Dumbarton. Duff's erratic performance was blamed on reveries the previous evening and resulted in his prompt dismissal from the club.

— CELTIC LEGENDS: BILLY McNEILL —

Billy McNeill: one of the greatest Celts of all time

The captain and inspirational defensive rock of Celtic's most successful side, Billy McNeill won more honours than any other player associated with the club and played in a record 790 games.

A 6ft-plus stopper who was imperious in the air and snapped into bone-jarring tackles with a ferocious determination, McNeill was also a supremely fair player – he received just a single red card in a career spanning two decades.

Although his name rarely appeared on the scoresheet, when

McNeill did find the net his goals tended to be vital. His dramatic late winner against Dunfermline in 1965, for example, secured the Scottish Cup in Jock Stein's first season in charge.

As with so many of the club's emerging prospects, McNeill's career took wing under Stein but he had been on the club's books for some years before the arrival of the man who was to transform his career.

Much was expected of McNeill from a young age. After signing schoolboy forms, he was farmed out to Blanytre Vics before returning to debut as an 18-year-old. He was appointed captain in 1963, two years after he had the misfortune to make his international debut in Scotland's excruciating 9–3 defeat against England at Wembley.

Under the tutelage of Stein, a poise was recovered by McNeill that had been ebbing. He became his manager's leader on the pitch. "One of the greatest Celts of all time, an inspiring captain and a model for every young footballer," Stein said of him.

Nicknamed Cesar, when McNeill lifted the European Cup in 1967 – his greatest moment in a Celtic shirt – he became Caesar, the conquering emperor of football.

He successfully led from the front in many more campaigns to bring his medal haul up to 22 – one fewer than Bobby Lennox, who was an unused sub on two occasions – before retiring, fittingly, after raising the Scottish Cup in 1975.

McNeill was a Celtic manager-in-waiting from that point. Cutting his teeth with Clyde before impressing with Aberdeen, his time came in 1978 when Stein was forced to make way after the club's poorest season in two decades. As he had as a player, McNeill galvanised the Celtic dressing room and won the title in his first season.

Regular trophy success followed until a dispute over wages caused McNeill to leave for Manchester City in 1983. He returned four years later with the Graeme Souness Rangers revolution in full swing. But once more showing himself a sharp operator in the transfer market, he inspired a remarkable turnaround to see Celtic claim the country's major honours as the club celebrated 100 years in existence. Thereafter, as Celtic struggled to keep pace with their free-spending rivals, McNeill's job proved impossible and he was sacked in 1991. However, he remains a revered figure among the club's fans.

Billy McNeill factfile

Born: Bellshill, 2nd March, 1940

Appearances: 790

Goals: 35

Full international appearances while at Celtic: 29 caps for
Scotland

Honours:

League championship: 1965/66, 1966/67, 1967/68, 1968/69,
1969/70, 1970/71, 1971/72, 1972/73, 1973/74

Scottish Cup: 1965, 1967, 1969, 1971, 1972, 1974, 1975

League Cups: 1965/66, 1966/67, 1967/68, 1968/69, 1969/70,
1974/75

European Cup: 1967

— A FAREWELL TO BE FOREVER REMEMBERED —

Those running the club often refer to 'the Celtic family' as a means
of encapsulating the countless numbers tied powerfully to a great
footballing institution through various links. In the modern day,
never has there been a more poignant illustration of these familial
bonds than the funeral of Tommy Burns.

The head of the club's youth development at the time of his
death from skin cancer at the age of 51, Burns was a great servant
to Celtic as player and manager. For his funeral on 21st May
2008, more than 20,000 lined the route from St Mary's Church in
the Calton – the birthplace of the club and where he grew up – to
Celtic Park for the passing of the cortège.

The turnout, which invited comparisons with the funeral of
goalkeeper John Thomson in 1931, spoke volumes about Burns's
personal standing. As his friend and former Celtic assistant Billy
Stark said in a moving eulogy at his requiem mass in St Mary's,
Burns touched people through his devotion to family, faith and
his football club. On a deeply affecting day, Rangers' management
team of Walter Smith and Ally McCoist were among the
pallbearers.

— BIG CROWD IN TODAY —

Celtic have always been a draw whose popularity has made them more than a big fish in Scotland's small pond. Indeed, their attendance highs are often not merely local bests:

- The 146,433 crowd that watched Celtic's Scottish Cup final win over Aberdeen on 24th April 1937 constitutes the largest attendance at a club match in Europe. It is believed more than 30,000 people were also locked out. If they had been somehow squeezed in, the figure would have threatened the world record set when 177,000 were shoe-horned in to the Maracana Stadium for a meeting between Brazilian rivals Flamengo and Fluminense in August 1963.

- In attracting 133,961 paying punters to Hampden Park, the second leg of the European Cup semi-final against Leeds United on 15th April 1970 was watched by the largest attendance ever for a tie in European competition.

- Celtic were the opposition when Rangers attracted a record 118,567 for a Scottish league game on 2nd January 1939. The same two clubs also set the Scottish League Cup record, 107,609 fans attending the League Cup final at Hampden on 23rd October 1965.

- The record attendance for Celtic Park is often given as 92,000 for a league match against Rangers on 1st January 1938. Yet contemporary reports give the figure as 83,500.

- The smallest crowd Celtic are believed to have played in front of for an official league match is the 1,000 that watched them play lowly Abercorn, a Paisley team, on 7th November 1896.

- Celtic's biggest attendance for a game since the stadium was fully redeveloped in 1998 is 60,632 for the visit of Manchester United in the Champions League on 21st November 2006.

- Celtic's lowest crowd for an SPL game is 3,567, the turn-out when they played Gretna at Livingston's ground on 23rd March 2008. A late switch from Gretna's temporary home at Fir Park and doubts over whether the game would go ahead were factors in the poor attendance.

— CELTIC LEGENDS: JIMMY JOHNSTONE —

The legendary 'Jinky' Johnstone

Among the legion of legendary Jimmy Johnstone tales, the essence of an entertainer endowed with gifts that should be beyond mere mortals is probably best captured in his reason for rampaging against Red Star Belgrade. The little winger, all 5ft 4in and nine-and-a-half stone of him, had a pathological fear of flying. With the score 1–1 after the first half of a European Cup tie at home to the Yugoslavians on 13th November 1968, he struck a deal with Celtic manager Jock Stein that if a decisive result was obtained he would be excused the long trip to Belgrade. Johnstone duly delivered a devastating display, scoring two of the goals and setting up the other three in a 5–1 win.

Breathtaking brilliance meets comedy meets insecurity. These elements jostle for attention in the football career and life of 'Jinky' – a football conjurer capable of sleight of foot and body and a flawed man whose sense of fun sometimes left him putting his foot in it. Stein was once asked for his greatest contribution to football. "I think that keeping Jimmy Johnstone in the game for so long was the best thing I ever did," he replied.

The greatest ever Celt, as voted by the club's fans in 2002, the long and painful battle with motor neurone disease that claimed Johnstone at the age of only 61 in 2006 meant for a time grins required to be tinged when recalling his days on this earth. But only briefly. Ultimately, it is impossible to think of Johnstone in a professional capacity and not respond in a gleeful way.

He was adored by supporters, especially those in the Jungle. He seemed just a wee red-headed boy doing impossible things and taking horrendous punishment from bruising defenders in the process. Johnstone was kicked to bits throughout his career. His distrust of authority meant he would not wait for referees to act in his defence but retaliate and he racked up a red-card count reflecting that.

A true street player, the one-time Celtic ball-boy honed his skills by running in miners' boots to build up his muscles and dribbling along the tops of walls to develop his control and balance. He had shown promise in the pre-Stein days but he flowered when the manager, who constantly had to employ carrot and big stick with him, moved him to outside right.

The French press dubbed him the Flying Flea after he buzzed all over Nantes in the course of Celtic's winning European Cup run of 1967. In later years, Johnstone would claim his best performance was in Alfredo Di Stefano's testimonial at Real Madrid's Bernabéu Stadium, a fortnight after Lisbon. Watched by a record 120,000, Johnstone was unstoppable. He beat five men to set up Bobby Lennox for the only goal. By the end his every touch was greeted by shouts of 'Olé!' from the crowd and at full-time the Real players clapped him off the field with a guard of honour.

His destruction of Terry Cooper, who described him as "my nightmare" in the European Cup semi-final second leg against Leeds United at Hampden in 1970 rivalled that Madrid masterclass. He was only 30 when freed by Celtic in June 1975 and thereafter did not have the same motivation in stints with San José Earthquakes, Sheffield United, Dundee, Shelbourne and Elgin City.

Johnstone's 23-cap total, as with so many Celtic players of that era, little reflects his talents. He claimed he never felt as comfortable in a Scotland shirt as for his club and never forgave the supporters of the national team for booing him because they favoured Rangers winger Willie Henderson. Yet he could still produce classic moments, not least when he gave England the runaround in 1974 at Hampden, three days after the infamous 'Largs boat incident' when, inebriated, he set sail on the Firth of Forth and had to be rescued by coastguards. Brilliance meeting comedy meeting insecurity all over again.

Jimmy Johnstone factfile
Born: Uddingston, 30th September 1944
Died: Uddingston, 13th March 2006
Appearances: 515
Goals: 130
Full international appearances while at Celtic: 23 caps for Scotland
Honours:
League championship: 1966/67, 1967/68, 1968/69, 1969/70, 1970/71, 1971/72, 1972/73, 1973/74
Scottish Cup: 1967,1971,1972,1974
League Cup: 1965/66, 1966/67, 1969/70, 1974/75
European Cup: 1967

— THE LIMP 11 —

It is perhaps no wonder that Celtic suffered a shocking loss to First Division Raith Rovers in the 1994 League Cup final. They were then in the midst of an 11-game run without a league win, the longest in their history. The dismal sequence began with a 2–2 draw away to Dundee United on 5th November 1994 and concluded with a 0–0 draw away to Aberdeen on 26th December that year.

— ALSO KNOWN AS —

Nicknames that don't involving simply shortening a player's name or adding a '–y' to it have been in short supply in the past decade or so. The one notable exception is current goalkeeper Artur Boruc. The Polish international is known universally as the Holy Goalie because of the kerfuffle made of him blessing himself in derby games at Ibrox. It is a worthy addition to a cannon of memorable soubriquets, which include:

The Wee Barra (Bobby Collins): A Glasgow reference to his squat frame.

Caesar (Billy McNeill): It should actually be Cesar since he was so called by teammates in his Celtic youth because he alone had a car, recalling Cesar Romero in the film *Ocean's Eleven*. His imperial comportment and leadership qualities meant the name morphed into Caesar.

Champagne Charlie (Charlie Nicholas): The forward's on the town, 'playboy' status made this moniker a tabloid gift.

The Duke (Sandy McMahon): He had a likeness to the Duke of Wellington.

The Hooded Menance ('Peter' McGonagle): Thought to come from a comic strip character, it was given to a 1930s full back reputedly intimidating in look and play.

The Human Torpedo (Jimmy McGrory): In recognition of his trademark diving headers.

Jinky (Jimmy Johnstone): He darted, he dribbled, therefore he jinked.

Lemon (Bobby Lennox): Given to him by teammate Willie Wallace after his name was mispelt in a newspaper.

The Maestro (Paul McStay): So dubbed because of his controlled, stand-out excellence.

Napoleon (Jimmy McMenemy): A nod towards his positional nous and ability to read situations.

Sunny Jim (Jim Young): So called after a character in an ad for a breakfast cereal.

— THE OLD FIRM AS FRIENDS . . .
AND FIERCEST FOES —

The term 'Old Firm', and the enmity for which it has become notation, are two distinct, and contrasting, entities. The Old Firm as an appellation was first coined in 1904, in a cartoon in *Scottish Referee*. It caricatured the financial carve-up of the Scottish game that the two, it was felt, were in cahoots over.

The clubs had the biggest supports in the country. The suspicion was that, in an amateur era, they cynically exploited the commercial appeal of their co-existence in the style of business partners rather than on-field rivals.

In the early days, the teams even shared train compartments when heading south for friendlies against English clubs, while Celtic treasurer John McLaughlin played piano at Rangers' social club.

With the advent of professionalism, each sought supremacy and the cordiality diminished, but it would be wrong to suggest the clubs then divided along ethnic and religious lines. Celtic grew out of Irish Catholicism of a republican hue, but crucially had no ban on players of any belief system. Rangers did not begin as a Protestant club. The policy of not knowingly signing Catholics emerged in the 1910s, as supporters began to affiliate themselves with the unionist cause in Ireland.

In 1912, Harland and Wolf opened a shipyard on the Clyde and imported an Irish Protestant workforce. The Orange Order were well represented among the new personnel who were antagonistic towards Catholics. Celtic were then the pre-eminent football club in Scotland and the newcomers' desire for a team to challenge these Irish Catholic upstarts saw them latch on to the nearby Govan club. Rangers' identity was irrevocably changed.

In short, if Rangers did not exist, Celtic's history would be unaltered. If Celtic did not exist, however, Rangers' history would be very different. The Ibrox club's embracing of Protestantism was a reaction to Celtic successfully existing.

After the First World War, the socio-political and socio-religious splits that characterised the Old Firm rivalry mutated into bigotry, sectarianism and a mutual loathing. These regularly spilled over into violence when the two tribes went to football war.

The conflict in Ireland certainly stoked the divisions; the

songbooks of both clubs offering slanted histories of the island. Supporters of each side adopted a ghetto mentality, but with Catholics a discriminated minority in Scotland and Rangers party to this at an institutional level, Celtic followers have always contended they are the victims of the divide.

Old Firm games may remain hate-filled spectacles but many believe there is now a degree of empty ritual in the bitterness that cascades from the stands. Rangers' disciminatory signing policy was ended when Mo Johnston became their first high-profile Catholic signing of the modern age in 1989. Since then the club have had both a Catholic captain and a Catholic manager.

Fergus McMann did much to tackle Celtic supporters' prejudices with his brave 'Bhoys Against Bigotry' campaign launched in 1996, and in recent years Rangers have followed suit with various laudable initiatives. Eradicating the "F*** the Pope" brigade, as Rangers owner David Murray has called the sectarian element of his support, has become imperative for his club after their fine from UEFA for "discriminatory chanting" in 2006.

Celtic chief executive Peter Lawwell is unapologetic about his club's support continuing to identify "strongly" with Ireland. He maintains that fan behaviour at Celtic home games is impeccable and that his club now have only a "narrow" problem he identifies as the away support giving voice to "offensive" songs – those celebrating the old IRA, the very force responsible for the formation of the Republic of Ireland.

But even with Scotland increasingly secular, disturbing elements can still rise to the surface in the Old Firm domain. When Celtic's Polish goalkeeper Artur Boruc revealed 'a God bless the Pope' T-shirt after the derby in April 2008, he was pilloried in the press for attempting to wind-up Rangers fans. Even if that was his intention, few stopped to question what it said about modern day Scotland – one nation, many cultures – that anyone's sensibilities could be offended by a Polish Catholic celebrating the only Polish Pope.

In the same season, with previous Ibrox favourite *The Billy Boys* becoming a proscribed song because it celebrates acts of violence against Catholics, a section of the Rangers support took to singing "the famine is over, why don't you go home". The couplet, a reference to the potato famine of the 18th century that brought the migration giving rise to Celtic is clearly racist and has been legally judged so.

— FIR PARK MISERY —

In a meaningless end of season fixture on 30th April 1937 Celtic
were thrashed 8–0 at Motherwell, the club's record defeat. For those
Celtic fans present at Fir Park it was hard to believe that the same
starting XI had only four days earlier beaten Aberdeen in the Scottish
Cup final in front of a record crowd. Perhaps the players hadn't
shaken off their hangovers before allowing an altogether different
sort to be inflicted.

— WE'RE NOT PARANOID, BUT . . . —

The belief of many involved with Celtic that Rangers are favoured
by the Scottish footballing establishment has even given rise to a
term, 'Celtic paranoia'. And some choice remarks:

"We have to recognise that most Lanarkshire referees, at least
90 per cent of them enter football, supporting or having supported
one member of the Old Firm . . . and there's no denying that. What
happens to a referee in the split-second that a player goes down in
the penalty area? If he is a Rangers supporter – and the player is a
Ranger – the referee . . . still sees that incident as a supporter . . .
It's human nature."
Celtic chairman **Bob Kelly** in his 1971 biography

"If it was up to me our application to join the English League would
be made tomorrow."
Celtic manager **Davie Hay** after a dubious penalty decision given
by referee David Syme in a 2–1 defeat by Rangers in the 1986 League
Cup final

"I was told when I joined this club about Celtic's paranoia – now
I know it's true. We are hard done by religiously and politically.
There are people against us . . . I meet people who hate me just
because I am the manager of Celtic."
Liam Brady after being appointed Celtic manager in 1991

"It's not that they weren't penalties – it's just that they are the kind
of penalties nobody else gets!"
Celtic fanzine *Not The View* after Rangers were awarded three
penalties in a 2–2 draw with Dundee in May 2003

"To get nine bookings? I think there's only one man to ask about that. It's time to start singing that old song again, 'That's why we're paranoid'."

Celtic manager **Gordon Strachan** after referee Mike McCurry cautioned nine Celtic players during Rangers' 3–0 win at Ibrox in October 2008

"These articles about me are written by, in my opinion, people who sympathise with Rangers. The Scottish media in general seems to favour our rivals. They are lauded for their feats in the UEFA Cup and in the league. I'm convinced if Celtic had been in the same situation there wouldn't be the same reaction."

Celtic goalkeeper **Artur Boruc** goes on the attack about Rangers bias in the media after he was slated for showing off a 'God Bless the Pope' T-shirt following an Old Firm win in April 2008.

— THE VIEW AND NOT —

In 1965, Celtic became the first football club in Britain to launch its own weekly newspaper. *The Celtic View* was the brainchild of Jack McGinn, then a supporter working in the circulation of Beaverbrook Papers. The success of the venture was to see him later become a club director then chairman.

The paper was given the go-ahead at a board meeting in March 1965 that was the first attended by new manager Jock Stein. He told McGinn to reserve a space on the front cover of the first issue – agreed for a publication date of 11th August 1965, to coincide with the start of the new season – for a picture of the team with the Scottish Cup . . . a competition the club hadn't won since 1954 and were then a game away from even reaching the final of. The space was duly filled.

As ought to be guessed from the title, *The Celtic View* takes the official club line. That has caused great disgruntlement over the years. As the old board became ever more discredited, this earned it the nickname *Pravda*, a reference to the state-controlled Soviet newspaper.

Believing *The* View did not provide a forum for supporter dissent and concerns, a group of 'malcontents' – the label given to disaffected fans by McGinn – created fanzine *Not The View* in 1987. Gloriously sharp and funny, it mercilessly lampooned its own club as much as the enemy Rangers, and quickly became the best-selling such publication in Britain, and a Celtic institution – as remains *The Celtic View*, now a glossy magazine.

— DARLING JOHNNY —

Before Celtic Park's main stand had an extension built onto it in the late 1980s, there were very few mementoes on show in the single wall of glass cabinets. Pride of place was given to John Thomson's Sunday School Bible and his goalkeeping top.

Thomson, it can be said, gave his life for Celtic. He became a martyr to the club's cause in the eyes of the supporters after an accidental collision with Rangers forward Sam English. Diving at English's feet five minutes into the second half of a game at Ibrox on 5th September, 1931, Thomson suffered fatal head injuries and was pronounced dead at Victoria Hospital in Glasgow at 9.25pm that evening. He was only 22. An unassuming lad from Fife, more than 30,000 people attended his funeral in his home town Carcarden. Many walked the 40 miles from Glasgow and slept out overnight to do so.

Untimely death can exaggerate the talents of even the gifted. It certainly lends a mawkish element to the memories of a man dubbed the Prince of Goalkeepers. It is Celtic supporters' way to drench themselves in sentiment, but Thomson does appear to have been the outstanding goalkeeper of his generation. He was signed by accident after Celtic scout Steve Callaghan was mesmerised by the figure "leaping like a cat" in the Wellesley Juniors goal, having gone to watch the opposing goalkeeper playing for Celtic Denbeath.

Thomson gained four full Scotland caps, claimed Scottish Cup winners medals in 1927 and 1931 and earned huge admiration for his grace and bravery. He raced out of his six-yard box to catch crosses and block at the feet of opponents in an era when keepers tended to be goal-line stoppers.

Regular pilgrimages are still made to Thomson's grave in Bowhill Cemetery, Cardenden and the song composed in his honour remains one of the most moving in the Celtic canon.

The John Thomson Song

A young lad named John Thomson,
From the Wellesley Fife he came,
To play for Glasgow Celtic,
And build himself a name.
On the fifth day of September,
'Gainst the Rangers club he played,
From defeat he saved the Celtic,
Ah but what a price he paid.
The ball came on, the centre too,
Young John ran out and dived,
The ball rolled by; but John lay still,
For his club this hero died.

I took a trip to Parkhead,
To the dear old Paradise,
And as the players came out,
Sure the tears fell from my eyes.
For a famous face was missing,
From the green-and-white brigade,
And they told me Johnny Thomson,
His last game he had played.

Farewell my darling Johnny,
Prince of players we must part,
No more we'll stand and cheer you,
On the slopes of Celtic Park.
The fans they all are silent,
As they travel near and far,
No more they'll cheer John Thomson,
That bright and shining star.
So play up Glasgow Celtic,
Stand up and play the game,
For in your goal a spirit stands,
Johnny Thomson is his name.

— FAMILY AT OLD FIRM WAR —

A number of brothers have taken up arms together in the Celtic cause to face Rangers. Only one set of brothers, though, have faced each other in Old Firm encounters – Celtic centre back Tom McAdam and Rangers centre forward Colin McAdam, who were on opposite sides between 1980 and 1981.

— UNFORGETTABLE GAMES: THE LANCING OF LEEDS —

Celtic 2 Leeds United 1, European Cup semi-final second leg, Hampden, 15th April 1970

This defeat of Leeds remains Celtic's finest performance after their Lisbon triumph. After laying the groundwork with a 1–0 win at Elland Road, Hampden was the scene for a captivating *coup de grâce* in front of a European record crowd of 136,505. The home and away victories over the English champions were all the sweeter because Leeds manager Don Revie had said five years earlier that Scottish football was going to be on its uppers by 1970.

Leeds took an unexpected lead when Billy Bremner hammered a thunderous 25-yard shot beyond Evan Williams after only 14 minutes. Celtic, though, stuck to their task and took a stranglehold through the running power of Bobby Lennox and Jimmy Johnstone, the pair fed by crisp, inventive passes from George Connelly, Bertie Auld and Bobby Murdoch.

Two minutes after the break, Auld swept in a centre that John Hughes, stepping in front of Jack Charlton, headed in from six yards. The goal had been planned on the training ground, Jock Stein remembering that Hughes had dominated Charlton in the air during recent Scotland-England internationals.

Just three minutes later the tie was sealed when a superb Celtic move sliced Leeds apart. It began when Murdoch picked out Johnstone on the right. As Terry Cooper and Norman Hunter edged across to double up on the man Stein had predicted would "destroy" Leeds, the winger dinked the ball into the space behind the two defenders. Collecting the return ball, Murdoch burst forward to drill in a low effort from the edge of the area past Leeds substitute keeper David Harvey.

Leeds barely threatened after that knock-out blow. Celtic's glorious achievement in reaching a second European Cup final inside three years was celebrated in style by their supporters, who stayed behind for 20 minutes after the final whistle until their heroes returned for a well-deserved lap of honour. Sadly, that was as good as it got for Celtic, who lost in the final to Feyenoord.

Celtic: Williams, Hay, Gemmell, Murdoch, McNeill, Brogan, Johnstone, Connelly, Hughes, Auld, Lennox

Leeds United: Sprake (Harvey), Madeley, Cooper, Bremner, Charlton, Hunter, Lorimer, Clarke, Jones, Giles, Gray

— OFF! OFF! OFF! OFF! —

Celtic's three matches with Racing Club of Argentina in the World Club Championship of 1967 have passed into football folklore as some of the most violent and bad-tempered ever played.

After Celtic won the first leg 1–0 at Hampden on 18th October, the sides met again a fortnight later for the second leg in Buenos Aires. Racing won 2–1 to set up a play-off four days later in Uruguay, but Celtic chairman Bob Kelly was so appalled by the cynical conduct of the Argentines he considered pulling his club out of the decider.

Despite Kelly's misgivings, the match at the Centerario Stadium in Montevideo on 4th November went ahead as planned. Under intense provocation from their opponents, Celtic cracked. For the only time in their history, four Celtic players – Bobby Lennox, Jimmy Johnstone, John Hughes and Bertie Auld – were dismissed, though Auld refused to go and played on for the full 90 minutes. Racing also had two players sent off by incompetent Paraguayan referee Perez Osorio, while fighting between the players led to police twice running onto the field to attempt to restore some semblance of order to a shameful scrap won 1–0 by Racing Club.

Having won such universal acclaim for the European Cup triumph four months earlier – a triumph that set them up for the home and away Inter-Continental Cup games against South America's champions – Celtic's global reputation was sullied by the spectacular loss of control.

— THE UPS AND DOWNS OF JORGE CADETE —

He was a flighty type of a different feather, was Portuguese international striker Jorge Cadete. Goals aplenty came in his short time at Celtic – 38 in 49 appearances – but so did moans. He joined in March 1996 and extricated himself from a contract he felt was unjust with a move to Celta Vigo in August 1997. In between, he claimed psychiatric problems prevented him returning to the club for the 1997/98 pre-season. Months earlier, he became so down about owner Fergus McCann's refusal to discuss an improved deal he bought a budgie he called Fergus to which he could pour out his troubles.

Controversy seemed to follow Cadete, even after he left Celtic Park. In 2002, he appeared on Portugal's *Big Brother* and began dating a pop star he met in the house called Nicole, formerly of Portuguese girl band Tentacoes. When he was eventually evicted he claimed the result was rigged.

If he wasn't going cuckoo by then, he definitely seemed to be two years later when, at the age 35 and 18 months after his last competitive game, he returned to Scotland to look for a club in 2004. Cadete seemed all set to sign for Raith Rovers and was even photographed in a Rovers' shirt, but changed his mind before he put pen to paper. Instead, he joined Partick Thistle, making his debut as a sub against Celtic. Recalling his messy departure from the club, the Celtic fans roundly booed him. After just a handful of games for the Jags he was on the move again, returning to Portugal to play for Deportivo Pinhalnovense.

— BARGAIN XI —

1. Ronnie Simpson (£2,000 from Hibernian, September 1964)
2. Didier Agathe (£35,000 from Hibernian, September 2000)
3. Bobo Baldé (free from Bordeaux, July 2001)
4. Pat Stanton (swap deal with Jackie McNamara, September 1976)
5. Andy Lynch (£35,000 from Hearts, February 1973)
6. Billy Stark (£75,000 from Aberdeen, July 1987)
7. Murdo MacLeod (£100,000 from Dumbarton, November 1978)
8. Lubo Moravcik (£350,000 from MSV Duisburg, October 1998)
9. Henrik Larsson (£650,000 from Feyenoord, July 1997)
10. Brian McClair (£75,000 from Motherwell, June 1983)
11. Joe McBride (£22,500 from Motherwell, June 1965)

— LARSSON'S LANDMARKS —

Henrik Larsson's scoring feats are the stuff of legend and legacy:

- He is the only player to have been top league goalscorer in Scotland on five separate occasions, achieving this feat in 1998/99, 2000/01, 2001/2002 and 2002/2003 and 2003/04. But for his leg break in October 1999, there is every reason to suspect he would have been leading scorer for six consecutive seasons.

- He reached the three-figure mark for league goals in fewer games than any player since the introduction of the Premier League in 1975, requiring only 116 league appearances to bring up the ton.

- Only Bobby Lennox, with 273 goals in 589 appearances, has found the net more often for Celtic in the post-war era than Larsson.

- In hitting hat-tricks in no fewer than 15 games, Larsson has netted more triples than any other Celtic player in the post-war era.

- The 53 goals Larsson netted for Celtic in season 2000/01 was the highest haul for a season in Scotland since Jim Forrest accumulated 57 for Rangers in the 1954/55 campaign. The Swede's total was the greatest by a Celtic player in the post-war era.

- The Golden Boot (for Europe's top scorer) earned by Larsson in 2000 made him the first Celtic player ever to earn such an accolade and the only player plying his trade outside one of Europe's big leagues to claim the trophy since ratings were weighted in favour of the more illustrious championships across the continent.

- His 35 league goals in the 2000/01 season saw him equal the record set by Brian McClair in 1986/87. McClair, though, bagged his total in a 44-game campaign while Larsson's came in a 38-match programme.

- Larsson is the only Scottish-based player ever to have scored in both the finals of the World Cup and the European Championships. He netted for Sweden against Italy in the 2000 European Championship finals in Holland and Belgium and scored three times – twice against Nigeria and once against Senegal – in the 2002 World Cup finals in Japan and South Korea.

- Larsson is way out in front as Celtic's leading post-war Old Firm goalscorer, with 15 strikes in the fixture.
- In the 27-year history of the Scottish Professional Footballers' Association Player of the Year awards, Larsson is the only player to be awarded the accolade twice – in 1999 and 2001.

— THE HAMPDEN RIOT —

On 17th April, 1909, Celtic met Rangers in the Scottish Cup final replay at Hampden in a match which has since entered the annals of shame. After a 1–1 draw the two sets of supporters expected extra time, but when the players failed to reappear suspicions mounted that the 'Old Firm' had contrived a second replay for another big payday.

Incensed, fans of both sides began to riot; not with each other, but in a combined effort. Bonfires were lit on the pitch and fire crews and police were pelted with bricks and stones. The cup was subsequently withheld, and the two supports' reputation for lawlessness whenever they met was born.

— CHEERIO WIM —

As is often the club's way, there was a sour postscript to Celtic's 1998 title success. Less than 48 hours after the league championship had been wrapped up with victory over St Johnstone at Celtic Park, manager Wim Jansen resigned after activating a get-out clause in his contract.

Although Jansen is the only Celtic manager to leave while the club were champions, his departure was not a complete surprise as it was public knowledge that he had a fractious relationship with Celtic chairman Fergus McCann and general manager Jock Brown. Jansen had also publicly admitted some months earlier that he was considering leaving the club.

— UNFORGETTABLE GAMES:
THE MOST UNFORGETTABLE —

Celtic 2, Inter Milan 1, European Cup final, National Stadium, Lisbon, 25th May 1967

The zenith of a 121-year history chock-full of glorious triumphs, Celtic's victory in the 1967 European Cup final elevated the Glasgow club into another footballing sphere and contributed hugely to the club's appeal around the world.

The triumph has lost none of its gloss in the four decades since Jock Stein and his players, all of whom famously hailed from within 30 miles of Celtic Park, became the first British winners of the competition. If anything, the legend of the Lisbon Lions grows with each passing year.

The style of Celtic's victory was remarkable. On a baking afternoon (the final kicked off at 5.30pm), Stein's men put Inter's stiffling defensive catenaccio system to the sword with a swashbuckling display of attacking football. Notching up 42 goal attempts, a total unparalleled in the history of the final, Celtic hammered at the wall Inter had erected in front of their goal. "Like the Dutch speeded up," was Jimmy Johnstone's apt description of Celtic's version of Total Football.

Stein had urged his players to perform "as if there were no more tomorrows". In Lisbon they did not let their manager down by dominating the final after Jim Craig needlessly stuck out a foot to halt Renato Cappellini's run into the box seven minutes in. German referee Kurt Tschenscher pointed to the spot and Sandro Mazzola coolly despatched the ball into the left hand corner of Ronnie Simpson's net.

Inter, as expected, attempted to sit on their lead, believing that the pale, scrawny Scots would wilt in the Iberian heat. But Celtic, willed on by their 15,000 fans and the majority of neutrals in the 56,000 crowd, proved to be the fitter team as well as the more technically adept.

Just before half-time a Bertie Auld shot rattled the bar. It could have been a sign that this wasn't going to be Celtic's day, but Stein told his players during the break that if they continued with their enterprising game plan, they would win.

Celtic's dominance was eventually rewarded after 62 minutes when a cutback from Craig was met on the run by Gemmell, who battered in a low drive from the edge of the penalty area. Celtic continued to press and probe in search of the winner and it arrived five minutes from the end, Chalmers nudging in a Murdoch piledriver beyond Inter keeper Sarti.

There was no way back for the Italians. At the final whistle Celtic supporters invaded the pitch in delight, leaving captain Billy McNeill to fight through the throng to go up to lift the trophy while his teammates were confined to their dressing room. Their work had been done by then, however, as succinctly expressed by John Rafferty in his report for *The Scotsman*: "In old Lisbon tonight, Celtic annihilated Inter Milan by a single goal."

Afterwards, Stein lavished praise on his team. "There is not a prouder man on God's Earth than me at this moment," said the man famously told he was "immortal" by Liverpool manager Bill Shankly in the Lisbon dressing room. "Winning was important, aye, but it was the way we won that has filled me with satisfaction. We did it by playing pure, beautiful, inventive football. There was not a negative thought in our heads. Inter played right into our hands. It's sad to see such gifted players shackled by a system that restricts their freedom to think and act. Our fans would never accept that sort of sterile approach. Our objective is always to try and win, and win with style."

Even Inter coach Helenio Herrera, who had waged a war of mind games before the final, acknowledged that the better side had won. "We can have no complaints. Celtic deserved to win . . . we were beaten by their force. Although we lost, the match was a victory for sport," he said.

Celtic: Simpson, Craig, Gemmell, Murdoch, McNeill, Clark, Johnstone, Wallace, Chalmers, Auld, Lennox
Internazionale: Sarti, Burgnich, Faccetti, Bedin, Guarneri, Picchi, Domenghini, Cappellini, Mazzola, Bicicli, Corso

— TALENT FOR BIAS —

BBC's *Fame Academy* head honcho Richard Park used to be a football commentator and sports reporter on Glasgow's Radio Clyde. Celtic manager Jock Stein thought so little of the broadcaster's impartiality he would refer to him as 'Ibrox Park'.

— WILLIE MALEY: A HALF CENTURY OF SERVICE —

Willie Maley: 30 trophies in 43 years

For the first 52 years of Celtic's existence, one man was largely responsible for shaping and moulding the club's development. As manager for 43 of those years, Willie Maley effectively created the club. A haul of 30 trophies as an autocratic team arbiter is testament to his outstanding contribution.

The son of a British Army sergeant, Maley was born in barracks in Newry, County Down in Ireland in 1868. His family resettled in Cathcart, Glasgow and he featured in the first Celtic team of 1888, alongside his brother Tom. A onetime Scottish 100-yard sprint champion, Willie proved a servicable halfback until he retired in 1897. However, it was in his post-playing days that Celtic were able to channel his many attributes to their greatest effect.

Maley had impressed as a diligent character with a capable mind in the printworks he joined at the age of 13. There he gained experience in various disciplines, among them accountancy, which made him the ideal candidate for secretary-manager when the club moved from committee selection for the team. He soon made an indelible mark on the club by changing the ethos. Previously big spenders who pilfered top players from other clubs, Maley's Celtic began developing raw talent and forging teams that were driven by this special bonding.

Aged 29 when he took over the running of the team, Maley's inexperience did not prevent him guiding Celtic to the championship in his first full season in charge. His approach to managing players reflected his army upbringing. He gave orders, demanded they be carried out to the letter, and would tolerate no dissent or indiscipline. Aloof and unapproachable, he did no coaching, was never even present at training and wouldn't talk to his players at half-time or full-time, preferring to watch games from the directors' box. It is said, indeed, that the Celtic players would only discover if they were in the team by reading the papers.

Team talks were anathema to him, but it seems he would give these on occasion. A record exists of one such talk before a game at Ibrox in 1921. "Play the ball from the whistle and keep playing it . . . do your very best . . . remember the old Celtic spirit . . ." was the extent of it. By then, however, his actions were speaking louder than any words.

Maley's eye for talent was instrumental in his ability to construct a team that won six consecutive titles between 1905 and 1910, the year of the club's first double. Such success prompted claims Celtic were then without equal in world football. Not until the Jock Stein era was this run of titles surpassed. Maley then built another imperious side that claimed the championship four straight years from 1914 and, during that run of success, set an unbeaten record that still stands.

In the mid-1930s players such as Jimmy McGrory and Jimmy Delaney made his third-era Celtic team once more title winners; the championship claimed in 1936 and 1938. Two years later, however, with Celtic bottom of the league, the 71-year-old Maley was forced to retire by the Celtic board, a move that left considerable bitterness.

A man of complexity, Maley was no gruff footballing ogre. He had a hinterland and a heart. A successful businessman, he owned one of Glasgow's most famous sporting establishments, the Bank Restaurant. He was also a devout pilgrim who made many trips to Lourdes and was renowned for many acts of immense generosity and willingness to help individuals and groups.

— MILLER MAKES A SCOTTISH GOAL —

After 19 group ties and ten scorers from nine different countries, Kenny Miller became the first Scot to score for Celtic in the Champions League with a penalty that secured the club a 1–0 win over FC Copenhagen on 26th September 2006.

— LENNON ENJOYS IBROX MORE THAN LE GUEN —

Neil Lennon enjoyed more league victories at Ibrox than Rangers manager Paul le Guen. The Celtic midfielder was on the winning side seven times in Old Firm games at the home of the club's rivals during his seven years with Celtic from 2000. In his ill-fated eight months in Scotland for the 2007/08 season, the Frenchman guided Rangers to just six home league wins.

— NUMBERS NAME GAME —

Dutch striker Jan Vennegoor of Hesselink is the Celtic player with most letters in his name. The shortest is believed to be Du Wei. The Chinese centre-back also had the shortest of Celtic careers. He played only 45 minutes competitively for the club; hauled off at half-time as the Gordon Strachan's side suffered a truly shocking Scottish Cup defeat away to Clyde in January 2006.

— FAMILY TREES —

Celtic players connected by bloodlines:

Brothers:

Tom (1888–91) and Willie Maley (1888–97)

Michael (1888–88) and Frank Dolan (1890–94)

Michael (1888–93) and Tom Dunbar (1890–91 & 1892–97)

James (1890–95) and John Devlin (1895–95)

Willie (1912–29) and Jimmy McStay (1920–34)

Frank (1930–35) and Hugh O'Donnell (1932–35)

John (1941–65) and Billy McPhail (1956–58)

Frank (1960–64) and Jim Brogan (1962–75)

George (1973–83) and John McCluskey (1976–79)

Willie (1979–87) and Paul McStay (1981–97)

Fathers and sons:

Patsy (1911–26) and Willie Gallacher (1937–49)

Jimmy (1902–20) and John McMenemy (1925–28)

John (1932–45) and John Divers (1956–66)

Jimmy (1888–97) and Frank Kelly (1918)

Mike (1953–60) and Mike Conroy (1978–82)

Steve (1959–71) and Paul Chalmers (1979–86)

Gordon (1971–72) and Gordon (1992–98) and Scott Marshall (1999)

Jackie (1972–75) and Jackie McNamara (1995–2005)

Andy (1973–80) and Simon Lynch (1999–2001)

Other relations:

- John Divers of the 1930s was the nephew of Patsy Gallacher and cousin of Willie Gallacher. His son John, therefore, is Patsy Gallacher's great-nephew.
- Brothers Willie and Paul McStay are great-nephews of brothers Willie and Jimmy McStay.
- Present-day defender John Kennedy is the great-nephew of Jimmy Delaney.

— PUT A WHITE SOCK IN IT —

At the start of the 1965/66 season, Jock Stein decided to change Celtic's socks to all white. Previously, the design had been green-and-white ringed, these replacing the black socks the club wore until the 1930s.

— UNFORGETTABLE GAMES: SEVEN PAST NIVEN —

Celtic 7 Rangers 1, Scottish Cup final, Hampden, 19th October 1957

No Celtic supporter grows up without hearing tales of, arguably, the club's most incredible victory. The '7–1 game', as it is simply known, stands not merely as Celtic's most thumping derby win, but remains the biggest ever winning margin in a major British cup final.

At a sun-kissed Hampden in front of a crowd of 82,293, Celtic played as if the football gods had planted the ultimate smacker on them. Players whose sleek talents were not in doubt, but who had produced these on the big occasions infuriatingly infrequently, clicked in devastating fashion. A rugged Rangers were run ragged by nimbleness and invention. So it was that Celtic retained a trophy they had won only for the first time the previous year, and scored a success thereafter celebrated in both song and verse.

The architect of an awesome 90 minutes was right half Willie Fernie. Time and again, he drilled his way into the Rangers rearguard and created unpluggable holes that allowed Charlie Tully's chicanery, Neil Mochan's left-wing play and Billy McPhail's aerial assaults to wreak terrible damage on their opponents. So mercilessly did hat-trick bagger McPhail destroy recently acquired Rangers centre half John Valentine that the afternoon's events effectively ended his Ibrox career.

One of McPhail's countless knockdowns proved the catylast for the calamities that would follow for Rangers, Sammy Wilson accepting the set-up to volley in a 23rd-minute opener. Having earlier had two efforts shudder the woodwork, Celtic were firmly in the groove by then. But not until half-time beckoned did they gain proper reward for their efforts, when Mochan zipped into the middle and battered a low shot into the net.

McPhail headed in a third shortly after the break, but Billy Simpson pulled one back before Celtic went on the rampage as Rangers gave up the ghost. Another header from McPhail in the 53rd minute made it 4–1, and the fifth duly arrived with a Mochan close-range finish 15 minutes later. McPhail completed his hat-trick by sliding a neat effort past keeper George Niven before he was brought down for Fernie to make it 7–1 from the penalty spot in the final minute.

The rout has become the stuff of legend. 'Seven past Niven' became the answer Celtic followers gave whenever any Rangers-supporting friend requested the time, while the triumph was immortalised in two song adaptations. At the time, calypso ditty *Oh Island in the Sun* was riding high in the charts and the Celtic fans were soon singing their own version: "Oh Hampden in the Sun, Celtic seven and the Rangers one". The enduring appeal of the stunning victory is reflected in the fact that as late as the 1970s Terry Jacks's hit *Seasons in the Sun* also became source material for another lyrical celebration revolving around the line "We had joy, we had fun, we beat Rangers 7–1".

Although the final was filmed, not all the goals were captured for posterity. The cameraman on duty that day forgot to remove his lens cap for the start of the second half after returning from a tea break. It hardly seems to matter when the events of that day have been passed down to subsequent generations of the club's faithful almost frame by frame.

Celtic: Beattie, Donnely, Fallon, Fernie, Evans, Peacock, Tully, Collins, McPhail, Wilson, Mochan

Rangers: Niven, Shearer, Caldwo, McColl, Valentine, Davis, Scott, Simpson, Murray, Baird, Hubbard

— BLOW AWAY THE BLUES —

With Hampden out of commission as the result of reconstruction, the last competitive goal scored in front of the Jungle was by Lee Richardson, a consolation for Aberdeen in their 2–1 Scottish Cup final defeat by Rangers on 29th May 1993.

So that Rangers supporters would not be the last fans to stand in the area, Celtic organised a 'Blow Away the Blues' evening the following Tuesday. On a wet night, and with the club at its lowest ebb for decades, a remarkable crowd of 19,316 turned out for a couple of charity matches, one involving the Lisbon Lions, and a last Jungle sing-song.

— FROM THE MOUTH OF McCANN —

Although he was often perceived as a sour individual, former Celtic chairman Fergus McCann possessed an acidic wit that manifested itself in some delicious references to films, books and sayings when the occasion demanded:

"The Three Amigos"
On the big screen, they were hapless bandits. To McCann, they were Celtic strikers Pierre van Hooijdonk, Jorge Cadete and Paolo Di Canio, who atempted to extort salary increases by crying to the press that the club's owner had reneged on (fictitious) verbal promises.

"Principles, sir? Sorry, I can't afford them."
From George Bernard Shaw's *Pygmalion*, McCann scofflingly recited this whenever it was suggested that he had to give in to monetary demands, even if he occupied the moral high ground in not doing so.

"Do you believe that stuff the old man was saying the other night at the Oso Negro about gold changin' a man's soul so's he ain't the same sort of man as he was before findin' it?"
A line from *The Treasure of Sierra Madre* McCann would recall when despairing at the greed of footballers and their agents.

"And all the stars that never were, are parking cars and pumping gas."
The couplet from the Bacharach and David song *Do You Know the Way to San José* McCann offered as a retort to a pressman who asked if he was worried about losing 'stars' on pre-contract agreements.

"The dog barks but the caravan moves on."
After the club's share issue was an outstanding success, McCann offered the old eastern proverb as a retort to those critics, chief among them ousted director Michael Kelly, who confidently predicted it was doomed to fail spectacularly.

During the building of the stand on the site of the old Rangers end, the increased height of the new structure brought complaints from the residents in the council houses directly behind it. They claimed the stand was causing interference with their television pictures and demanded compensation. McCann said he would make a payment to all those who brought their TV licences up to the club. None ever did.

In the old Celtic Park, there was an 'unemployed gate', offering reduced admission to a standing area for those out of work. It was scrapped when the club returned to their all-seater stadium and McCann was chided for this at a meeting with supporters. He responded, "Do Tennent's have an 'unemployed' lager?"

— O'NEILL'S OUTSTANDING RECORDS —

Many of the feats Celtic achieved in the Martin O'Neill era are unlikely to be surpassed:

- Celtic's 25-game league winning run in 2003/04 is the longest victorious sequence in the 117-year history of Scottish top-flight football.
- Between losing 1–0 to Ajax in the return leg of a Champions League qualifier on 22nd August 2001 and a 2–1 defeat by Aberdeen in the league on the 21st April 2004, Celtic strung together a 77-game unbeaten home run, the longest by a top-flight Scottish club.
- Celtic lost only 15 of the 190 Premier League games they played under O'Neill. Four of these defeats came after the league was won.
- Celtic's 103 points total from the 2001/02 campaign is the best achieved in the Scottish top flight. In that season they only dropped two points at home . . . and repeated that feat the following season.
- O'Neill is the only Celtic manager to preside over seven straight Old Firm victories. The sequence included a 100 per cent record in the five meetings between clubs during the 2003/04 campaign – the club's first seasonal green-and-white wash of their ancient adversaries since 1971/72:

Date	Competition	Result
27th April 2003	League	Rangers 1 Celtic 2
4th Oct 2003	League	Rangers 0 Celtic 1
3rd Jan 2004	League	Celtic 3 Rangers 0
7th Mar 2004	Scottish Cup 4th rd	Celtic 1 Rangers 0
28th Mar 2004	League	Rangers 1 Celtic 2
8th May 2004	League	Celtic 1 Rangers 0
29th Aug 2004	League	Celtic 1 Rangers 0

CELTIC LEGENDS: JIMMY McGRORY —

Celtic's greatest ever goalscorer

The genial can be giants. Jimmy McGrory towers above all other goalscorers in the club's history. Yet, he can lay claim to being a singular Celt not merely for an unrivalled net-bulging record, but because he achieved it in so self-effacing a fashion. Character has always mattered in how Celtic's fabled servants have been judged.

McGrory was both an ordinary man and a football man to be loved. Even if his two decades as manager in the immediate post-war period produced desperate times, and a desperate undermining of an all-too-decent sort.

His commitment and courage in maximising a divine instinct for finding the net affords reverence. It brought him a record of 468 strikes in only 445 first-class appearances – a 15-year career of peerless plundering following his debut in 1923 that earned him the tag 'goal a game McGrory'. Such stats are all the more extraordinary because the Celtic teams he played for were of wildly varying quality.

His efforts were always of the highest order. They often seemed to defy the laws of physics. For though he was stocky, or perhaps because he was so – with thick neck and shoulders – his aerial prowess was astonishing. He would fearlessly dive headlong to meet any ball into the box, hanging in the air as if held up by an invisible force.

"They didnae lace up Jimmy's boots before a game, they laced up his heid," said fellow 1920s forward Tommy McInally. "He could hit the ball further with his head than some could with their boots," said 1930s teammate Jackie Watters. The greatest header in the history of the Scottish game, Queen's Park keeper Jack Harkness once broke three fingers trying to stop a bullet from his bonce. Strangely, his talents were little utilised at international level despite his seven Scotland appearances bringing six goals.

McGrory was raised in the tough Glasgow area of Garngad and signed for Celtic at the age of 18 from junior club St Roch's in 1922. He did so reluctantly because he was not convinced he was good enough. But a wage was important to a teenager who was required to provide financial support for his seven siblings, his mother having died when he was 12. On 30th August 1924 he attended his father's funeral but played and scored in a victory over Falkirk that afternoon. It was to set him on his way to being the club's top scorer that season and cement his place in a team to which he gave everything.

Celtic's treatment of McGrory in return was despicable. The club have often had a shameful habit of exploiting or mistreating those whose devotion to them is total, and McGrory fell into that category.

In 1928 manager Willie Maley attempted to sell him to Arsenal to pay for a new stand. The London club offered McGrory a three-time salary increase but he had no desire to play for any other club than Celtic. Rather than rewarding McGrory's loyalty, the club reacted to being denied a British record transfer fee by secretly paying him less than his teammates for the next decade.

He became Kilmarnock manager only two months after retiring as a Celtic player in 1937. The Ayrshire club closed during the duration of the Second World War but when the conflict ended the Celtic board agreed he was the perfect replacement for their second manager, Jimmy McStay.

Before being replaced by Jock Stein in 1965, the pipe-smoking McGrory enjoyed some fine successes: notably, the 1953 Coronation Cup triumph, a double the following year and the 7–1 victory over Rangers in the 1957 League Cup final. But as the club went into serious decline in the early 1960s he was considered too easily manipulated on team selection by chairman Bob Kelly and overall lacking in the required 'nasty streak'. What might have counted against him, then, will be forever recognised as an outstanding virtue.

Jimmy McGrory factfile
Born: Glasgow, 26th April 1904
Died: Glasgow, 20th October 1982
Appearances: 445
Goals: 468
Full international appearances while at Celtic: 7 caps for Scotland
Honours (player):
League championship: 1925/26, 1935/36
Scottish Cups: 1925, 1931, 1933, 1937
Honours (manager):
League championship: 1953/54
Scottish Cup: 1951, 1954
League Cup: 1956/57, 1957/58
St Mungo's Cup: 1951
Coronation Cup: 1953

— UNFORGETTABLE GAMES: ONE IN TEN —

Celtic 2 St Johnstone 0, 9th May 1998, Premier Division, Celtic Park

If the Hoover Dam ever burst it could not produce the sort of outpouring witnessed cascading down from the stands of Celtic Park at 28 minutes past four on the final afternoon of the 1997/98 league season. That was the time Harald Brattbakk knocked in a clinching second goal for Celtic that ensured the league championship would be theirs after a decade-long separation from the major honour.

But that is not how Celtic supporters choose to remember an emotion-drenched occasion. They will forever recall 9th May 1998 as the day they stopped Rangers "getting ten-in-a-row", and so prevented their bitter rivals usurping Jock Stein's precious nine consecutive titles. Sometimes it almost seems that their own club being title winners again, an achievement many had thought would remain long out of reach, was a side issue.

In a topsy-turvy season, Celtic were under new, unfancied coach Wim Jansen. With a dramatically recast squad, they began as rank outsiders for the championship. Over the winter months, a surge to the league summit made them odds-on favourites, even as the club was riven by internal division. But as both Old Firm clubs stumbled in the closing weeks, Celtic simply couldn't put Rangers away. Even when the Ibrox side gave the impression they just wanted to be put out of their misery; their previous summer's record spending spree failing to prevent Walter Smith's team exhibiting battle fatigue.

After Rangers lost at home to Kilmarnock in their penultimate game, Celtic had the opportunity to clinch the title a day later with a win at Dunfermline. Instead, the loss of a late equaliser brought a nervy draw. Going into their final game at home to St Johnstone, then, Celtic had to win to be sure that Rangers could not overtake them by claiming all three points away to Dundee United.

The mood was expectant, if edgy, inside a sunny Celtic Park. The noise level created at kick-off was full. Within two minutes it reached deafening proportions, after Larsson weaved in from the left and sent a curling, dipping tracer-bullet of a shot beyond Alain Main from the edge of the area. As he had been all that season, the Swede proved the blowtorch to fire the team's burning desire.

Celtic were determined not to sit on a lead, as had cost them at

Dunfermline and in some of their later league games. But St Johnstone held firm in the face of an onslaught and 50,000 Celtic hearts leapt into mouths when an unmarked George O'Boyle contrived to head over from six yards just minutes before the interval.

With Rangers winning 1–0 against United, Celtic needed the insurance of a second goal. But as the second half wore on they were beset by anxiety and looked increasingly less likely to find it until a well-worked move allowed Brattbakk to side-foot in a 74th-minute clincher. It seemed as if not ten but 100 years of frustration, upset, anger and fear were poured into the manic celebrations. Their eardrum-splitting force was so intense referee Kenny Clark simply picked the ball up to signal full-time rather than blowing a whistle that would never have been heard.

This was the moment a club was palpably reborn. It was also a vindication of owner Fergus McCann's efforts to rebuild and restructure a club he had saved from oblivion. A pivotal juncture in the club's history, the 1998 title success crucially allowed Celtic to rid themselves of an inferiority complex that had threatened to diminish them permanently.

Celtic: Gould, Boyd, Annoni, McNamara, Rieper, Stubbs, Larsson, Burley, Donnelly, Lambert, O'Donnell

St Johnstone: Main, McQuillen, Preston, Sekerlioglu (Griffin), McCluskey, Whiteford, O'Halloran (McMahon), O'Neil, Grant (Connolly), O'Boyle, Jenkinson

— McGRORY STRIKES FOR THE RECORD —

Some of Jimmy McGrory's scoring feats will surely never be beaten.

- On 14th January 1928 he netted eight of the goals in a 9–0 win over Dunfermline.
- He bagged a three-minute hat-trick in a 5–0 home win against Motherwell on 14th March 1936.
- McGrory scored four headers in a five-goal haul that brought a 6–2 win over Aberdeen on 23rd October 1926.
- In season 1935/36, he netted an incredible 50 league goals.

— 'WORSE THAN THE HUN' —

Many explanations are given as to why Celtic supporters call their ancient adversaries Rangers 'the Huns'. The nickname is the subject of much myth and legend. It appears a matter of taking your pick when it comes to deciding which source is most plausible.

It is curious, though, that the unflattering appellation has been co-opted into the debate over sectarianism – curious because it has no religious basis and, indeed, is believed to have been first used by Rangers fans as a label for their Celtic counterparts. "Worse than the Hun" was a phrase commonly used in the post-war era to describe anyone, or anything, considered beyond the pale. To followers of the Ibrox club their rivals' Irish origins made them a snug fit for the term since Ireland's neutrality in the Second World War was largely condemned as a tacit acceptance of Hitler's brutal empire building.

How 'the Hun' came to change sides is debatable but it occurred during the 1960s. Some say it happened after rioting by Rangers fans during a game in England led to a local paper running with a headline that the havoc wreaked was, you've guessed it, "worse than the Hun". On a similar theme, it is claimed that after several more violent excursions south of the border by Rangers fans, *The Daily Express* stated that the continent had not seen such rampaging since the days of Attila the Hun. One Celtic website now simply describes 'Huns' as right-wing fans of any club.

Whatever the truth, Scottish football supporters who abhor the Old Firm's religious zealotry are not averse to referring to Rangers as 'the Huns' – much to the chagrin of those so termed. As recently as early 2008, the Rangers Supporters' Trust demanded action be taken against St Mirren fans under the Scottish Premier League's recently introduced unacceptable conduct guidelines after they indulged in the traditional Celtic chant of "Go home ya Huns" during a match in Paisley. Followers of St Mirren, it must be said, have no form in the bigotry stakes.

— CRUM MAKES AN EXHIBITION OF HIMSELF —

It cannot be stated with certainty, but the final of the Empire Exhibition trophy in 1938 is cited by reliable historians as marking the first ever outlandish goal celebration by a Celtic player.

The tournament was devised to bring a football element to the opulent Empire Exhibition in Glasgow's Bellahouston Park. It became a British championship, to all intents and purposes, with Celtic, Rangers, Aberdeen, Hearts, Everton, Brentford, Chelsea and Sunderland featuring as the best of Scottish and English football in a knock-out competition held at nearby Ibrox.

It was clearly worth winning and Johnny Crum certainly thought so. In those days, goalscorers simply raised a hand and quickly ran back to their own half while exchanging handshakes with teammates. But in the 10th June 1951 final, before an 82,000 crowd that pitted Celtic (winners against Sunderland and Hearts) against Everton (victors over Rangers and Aberdeen) Crum netted an extra-time winner and then treated the crowd to a bit of jiggling and hip-swivelling behind the goal. He was about four decades ahead of his time.

— THROWING AWAY FOUR JACKS —

It was a quick throw-in what did it; or rather undid Dariusz 'Jacki' Dziekanowski's efforts on a night he became the only Celtic player to score four goals in a European tie. The British forward's quartet on 27th September 1989 seemed to have put the club on course to overturn a 2–1 deficit in the home return leg of their first round Cup Winners' Cup tie against Partizan Belgrade.

In a remarkable see-saw encounter, Celtic recovered from the loss of the opening goal to tie the aggregate scores at 3–3, before twice shaking off further setbacks to go 5–3 in front on the night with Dziekanowski's fourth goal nine minutes from time.

Then, inexplicably, defender Anton Rogan naively, nay preposterously, rushed to take a quick throw-in – learning nothing from the visitors' earlier time-wasting. Possession was quickly lost and Partizan raced up the park to score the goal that made it 6–6 on aggregate and put them through on the away goals rule. "We climbed three mountains . . . then proceeded to fall off them," Celtic manager Billy McNeill despaired afterwards. Dziekanowski, a £400,000 signing that summer, was never the same player again.

— CELTIC LEGENDS: BOBBY LENNOX —

'Celtic has been my life'

The greatest post-war Celt in so many ways, Bobby Lennox was the quickest, most lethal, most decorated, most effervescent club legend of the modern era, and the last Lisbon Lion to hang up his boots. His effectiveness was underpinned by a truly infectious *joie de vivre* and his champagne personality accounts for the great affection in which he is held.

"Celtic has been my life," he has said of a passion that never waned in the man justifiably labelled 'Evergreen', and who only quit at the age of 37 because surgeons told him he had no option. That was in 1980, a year after he returned from a brief spell with US side Houston

Hurricanes to add a Scottish Cup winners' medal to a collection that boasts 23 such badges, though two of these he picked-up after remaining on the bench in the 1972 and 1974 Scottish Cup finals.

Lennox came through the club's leanest period to feast on the fattest of fat that his fitness, dedication, bravery and composure in front of goal deserved. Yet, like many who arrived of the supremely talented crop that cut their teeth at Celtic in the early 1960s, his career appeared directionless until the arrival of Jock Stein in 1965. A native of Saltcoats who was signed from Ardeer Recreation in 1961 at the age of 18, the slight, wispy forward, became a scoring machine after Stein converted him from an orthodox left-winger to an inside left.

"Bobby would chase paper on a windy day," said fellow Lion Bertie Auld, the midfield schemer whose passes would spring Lennox into a blur of motion. The 'Buzzbomb', as he was nicknamed, would have detonated in the opponents' box on far more occasions than the 273 times he did – an astonishing Celtic record considering he was not strictly a striker – but for the fact he was all too often wrongly judged offside by linesmen he was simply too quick for. One such error ruled out a last-minute equaliser against Liverpool at Anfield in the 1966 Cup Winners Cup semi-final that would have progressed Celtic to a first European final.

Late strikes were a Lennox speciality because of his ability to outpace and outlast opponents. His constant running in the oppressive heat of Lisbon was a significant factor in Celtic pulling apart Inter to capture football's ultimate club prize in 1967. It capped a memorable two months for Lennox, who became a European winner only a few weeks after scoring as Scotland's modern-day Wembley wizards inflicted a first defeat on world champions England.

In the late 1960s Arsenal manager Bertie Mee was willing to pay a British record fee to capture Lennox but the player's bond with Celtic meant he could not be enticed south. He did not lack admirers in England, however. After a typically exuberant performance in the testimonial of Liverpool defender Ron Yeats testimonial in May 1974, Bobby Charlton, who had previously described him "as one of the best strikers I have ever seen" was moved to say: "If I'd had Lennox in my team, I could have played for ever."

It seemed as if Lennox would play for ever as, even in the twilight of his career, his pace was still a genuine weapon. He helped Celtic to the title in 1978/79 as an impact player by coming off the bench and scoring a handful of important goals and, after 15 goals in 36 games in America, returned for a Scottish Cup final hurrah in 1980. On retiring, he became reserve teach coach, a position he held for more than a decade. Lennox remains a regular visitor to Celtic Park and a matchday host, and still seems to have that old zip as he moves between corridors.

Bobby Lennox factfile
Born: Saltcoats, 30th August 1943
Appearances: 589
Goals: 273
Full international appearances while at Celtic: 10 caps for Scotland
Honours:
League championship: 1965/66, 1966/67, 1967/68, 1968/69, 1969/70, 1970/71, 1971/72, 1972/73, 1973/74, 1978/79
Scottish Cup: 1965, 1967, 1969, 1971, 1972, 1974, 1977, 1980
League Cup: 1965/66, 1966/67, 1967/68, 1968/69
European Cup: 1967

— CIVIL IN SEVILLE —

Celtic supporters have a rare ability to feast on failure. When asked about the achievement of reaching the 2003 UEFA Cup final in Seville, Martin O'Neill always finished with the same final words: "Ultimately, we lost. That's it." But that's not it for the 80,000 Celtic supporters who revelled in making the pilgrimage to Andalucía for the club's first European final in 33 years.

There were minor, but significant, triumphs amidst the major disappointment of the 3–2 extra-time defeat – a loss the Celtic faithful have always wrongly ascribed to Porto's desperate play-acting and pathetic time-wasting tactics. The conduct of Celtic's followers in Seville earned them fair play awards from both FIFA and UEFA, a rare double in the history of the game. It doesn't make up for events on the field, however many Celtic fans will claim May 22nd 2003 as one of the greatest nights of their lives.

— AWAY WITH THE FAIRIES —

Celtic have had some truly shocking change/away strips over the years. The colours to feature most often have been yellow, black, white and various shades of green.

- A green-and-white quartered jersey was tried out in the 1920s. Thirty years later, fans approved of a white jersey with green sleeves and facing, and a shamrock over the left breast.
- In 1973/74, the *Celtic View* ran a competition giving fans the chance to design an alternative strip. It was worn twice in the later part of that season and thereafter seemingly abandoned.
- Celtic fans were generally unimpressed by the all-white, the all-green and especially the all-yellow efforts their team used to wear when there was a colour clash. Only a black-and-green vertical striped design, Italian in look, was generally approved, and this was revived in 2006/07.
- As with the home kit and the club itself, the 1990s was a time to forget for Celtic change strips. Some were garish – such as a green-paint explosion/forest thicket number, a green stripes monstrosity or a bright yellow/tiger suit effort – to the point of being utterly putrid. The lack of subtlety was put down to the desire to crack the leisurewear market by Umbro, Celtic's long-time kit suppliers.
- The club's switch to a lucrative deal with Nike in 2005 has resulted in more tasteful designs . . . as well, seemingly, as a faster turnaround of alternative strips. As with many big clubs, three seem to run at any one time, and most have little more than an 18-month shelf life.

— OUT OF THE JUNGLE —

In the 1980s, the repertoire of the Jungle-ites was probably at its most inventive, offensive and unrepentant. Take your pick into which category the following, more memorable chants, would be placed:

"The Pope's coming over, oh yes the Pope's coming over."
Inspired by a first Scottish papal visit in 1982

"Argentina es Malvinas!"
A bold expression of support for Argentina during the 1982 Falklands conflict

"Michael Fagin shagged yir Queen!"
Thoughts on a Palace intruder

"Maggie, we nearly got you!"
Reaction to Prime Minister Margaret Thatcher's lucky escape in the IRA's bombing of the Grand Hotel in Brighton, 1984

"Arthur Scargill, Arthur Scargill!"
The 1984 miners' strike leads to an unexpected name being bawled from the enclosure

— ANOTHER HAMPDEN RIOT —

Celtic won the 1980 Scottish Cup final against Rangers at Hampden with an extra-time strike by George McCluskey, but it is for the post-match scenes that the 10th May encounter is seared into the Scottish public's consciousness.

After Celtic had paraded the trophy the two sets of fans became embroiled in a pitch battle, attacking each other in waves as truncheon-wielding mounted police attempted to restore order. Among the many appalling sights was that of a disabled supporter being thrown to the ground so his wheelchair could be added to the weaponry of bottles and wooden terracing supports. Beamed live across Scotland, the drink-fuelled savagery led to a ban on alcohol in Scottish grounds and the introduction of stricter measures to deal with the public disorder that many Old Firm confrontations produced.

— STEIN'S SAYINGS —

Jock Stein was a football laureate in his capacity for self-expression. By turns supremely insightful, puckishly humourous and affecting, he never seemed lost for the right words:

"Down there for eight hours you're away from God's fresh air and sunshine and there is nothing can compensate for that. There is nothing as dark as the darkness down a pit, the blackness that closes in on you if your lamp goes out. You'd think you could see some kind of shapes but you can see nothing, nothing but the inside of your head. I think everyone should go down the pit at least once to learn what darkness is."
Stein on being a miner

"It is up to us, everyone at Celtic Park now, to build our own legends. We don't want to live with history, to be compared to legends from the past. We must make new legends."
On winning his first league championship in 1966

"I cannot say that Celtic was my first love, but it will certainly be my last."
A reference, perhaps, to his Rangers-supporting background

"When we won the semi-final of the European Cup, I remember Kenneth Wolstenholme saying 'We've made it'. We became British that night. I don't mind that because I like to see the British game being successful. But I'd prefer to see the Scottish game successful."
On Celtic's European success

"An astonishing, coincidental coming together of great players, the likes of which we'll never see again."
Stein downplays his own role in moulding the Lisbon Lions

"Well, I don't know what they expect us to do next."
On fan expectations after the European Cup win

"Celtic jerseys are not for second best. They don't shrink to fit inferior players."
On the exacting standards he required of his players

"We'll wear the red stockings. Under the floodlights they show up more orange than red and our supporters will think that we're wearing the colours of the Irish tricolour. That'll please them."

After Celtic were ordered to dispense with their white socks and wear blue or red for the first leg of their 1970 European Cup semi-final against Leeds at Elland Road

"They have laughed at our football long enough down here. I am not talking about Leeds United or Don Revie; they have respect for us. I'm talking about the critics and commentators who have rarely given credit to Scottish football. Maybe tonight's result will stop them laughing."
On the 1–0 win that was the result of the above game

"We must not be too clever – we must only be clever."
On his approach to the game

"Football without the fans is nothing."
Keeping in mind the importance of Celtic's support

"If Celtic do well on the field it will not be worth it if their supporters cannot or will not behave decently."
His reaction to Celtic fans rioting after a pre-season friendly in Sunderland in the summer of 1965

"You are still saying all the right things, but they're just not listening as much."
On his miserable final season at Celtic in 1977/78

"We all end up yesterday's men in this business. You are very quickly forgotten."
On the perils of management

— JINKY EGG-STRA SPECIAL —

Shortly before he died, Jimmy Johnstone had an honour bestowed on him previously reserved for Russian rulers of the past. In June 2005 Fabergé designed an egg in recognition of the Celtic winger, making him the first living person to receive such treatment since the tsars. The work of Carl Fabergé's granddaughter Sarah, the egg was unveiled at the House of Commons in June 2006. A total of 19 were made and the entire limited edition collection sold out within days.

— WILLIE MALEY SONG —

Manager for a record 43 years between 1897 and 1940, Willie Maley is celebrated in song by the Celtic supporters to a tune which is borrowed from the 1978 hit *Matchstick Men and Matchstick Cats and Dogs* by Brian & Michael:

Willie Maley Song

Oh Willie Maley was his name,
He brought some great names to the game,
When he was the boss at Celtic Park.
Taught them how to play football,
He made the greatest of them all,
Gallagher and Quinn have left their mark.

Chorus

And they gave us James McGrory and Paul McStay,
They gave us Johnstone, Tully, Murdoch, Auld and Hay,
And most of the football greats,
Have passed through Parkhead's gates,
All to play football the Glasgow Celtic way

In '38 there was a show,
And Glasgow was the place to go,
A model of the Tower was football's prize.
England sent four of the best,
They didn't meet with much success,
Because the trophy ended up in Paradise.

Chorus

Well Coronation time was here,
'53, that was the year,
Another four from England met their doom.
They said we'll have to try again,
But like before it was in vain,
Because the Cup is in the Parkhead trophy room.

Chorus

Well 14 years had gone and so,
To Portugal we had to go,

To play the team that Italy adored.
Celtic went out to attack,
They won the Big Cup and they brought it back,
The first time it had been on British shores.

Chorus

Now 21 years to that day,
With pride, It's our centenary,
And we're among the honours once again.
Six million pounds the Huns did spend,
But Souness found it was in vain,
Because the Celtic are the Champions again.

Chorus

And now in 1995,
It feels good to be alive,
And we're about to celebrate again.
The fans all cry out for Pierre,
He rises up into the air,
And brings the Scottish Cup to Paradise.

Chorus

— THE ROAD TO LISBON —

Celtic's route to the final of the European Cup in 1967 saw them take on and beat some fine sides:

Round	Date	Result
1st	28th Sept	Celtic 2 Zurich 0
	5th Oct	FC Zurich 0 Celtic 3
2nd	30th Nov	Nantes 1 Celtic 3
	7th Dec	Celtic 3 Nantes 1
Qf	1st Mar	Vojvodina 1 Celtic 0
	8th Mar	Celtic 2 Vojvodina 0
Sf	12th April	Celtic 3 Dukla Prague 1
	25th April	Dukla Prague 0 Celtic 0
Final	25th May	Celtic 2 Inter 1

— THE CHANGING FACE OF CELTIC PARK —

In the weeks following Celtic's formation, volunteers set about creating a football ground on a vacant lot between London Road and Dalmarnock Street next to Janefield Street Cemetery. The result was a state-of-the-art ground boasting a level playing field, terracing and dressing rooms. The success of the park was ultimately its downfall when the landowner, on seeing the crowds of paying spectators, upped the rent by 800 per cent from £50 to £450 per annum.

The club then began the search for a new home. They found it just 500 yards away at a disused brickyard also on Janefield Street. Again, volunteers were called on to make ready the park, which was opened on 13th August 1892 at a Celtic Sports event. The updated version included a playing field, athletic and cycling tracks, a 15-tiered stand and pavilion.

The ground was soon dubbed 'Paradise' by the fans, the nickname stemming from the relative opulence of the club's new home and the departure from the nearby graveyard. Through the 1980s and early 1990s it wasn't always certain that Parkhead would remain Celtic's home. Questions about the appropriateness of building huge stands on the original site led to the old board, in their final desperate act, floating a hare-brained scheme to move the club to a toxic site in Cambuslang. The funding was supposed to be provided by a Swiss bank who ran a mile from the proposal in a turn of events crucial to Fergus McCann's February 1994 takeover. The current stadium still stands on the former brickyard.

Important dates and developments at Celtic's home:
1895 Turnstiles are installed at Celtic Park for the first time.
1897 Celtic Park stages the World Cycling Championships.
1898 First 'luxury' stand added.
May 1904 The main Janefield Street stand and pavilion are destroyed in a fire and replaced at a cost of £6,000.
1914 Park capacity increased to 25,000 following conversion of the cycle track to terracing.
1927–29 Another fire destroys the pavilion. The Grant Stand is demolished.
1957 West terracing has cover added.
Oct 1959 Floodlights are switched on at Celtic Park for the first time.

1964 Celtic Pools launched to provide revenue for the ground.

1966 The Jungle is renovated.

1968 East terracing is renovated.

1971 The main stand is renovated, and has a new capacity of 8,686.

1986 Following the re-roofing of the Celtic End, the entire ground becomes covered.

1988 The main stand receives a facelift and hospitality services are added.

April 1992 A move from Parkhead to a new 52,000 capacity stadium in Cambuslang is announced by the Celtic board.

June 1993 The end of the Jungle. It becomes a seating area for one season.

March 1994 New owner, Fergus McCann, confirms that Celtic Park will be upgraded to a 60,000-capacity stadium in the club's original East End home.

1994/95 Hampden becomes Celtic's home for the season.

Aug 1995 Rod Stewart opens the North Stand.

Aug 1996 The Lisbon Lions stand is opened.

Aug 1998 The Jock Stein stand is opened.

— UNBEATEN SEASON —

In 1897/98 Celtic went through the whole of the league season unbeaten, winning 15 and drawing three of 18 matches. The team's excellent form allowed them to claim the title by four points from Rangers. Celtic's results were as follows:

Opposition	Result home	Result away
Dundee	Won 2–1	Won 2–1
Hearts	Won 3–2	Drew 0–0
Hibernian	Won 4–1	Won 2–1
Partick	Won 3–1	Won 6–3
Rangers	Drew 0–0	Won 4–0
St Bernard's	Won 5–1	Won 2–0
St Mirren	Won 3–0	Drew 0–0
Third Lanark	Won 4–0	Won 1–0
Clyde	Won 6–1	Won 9–1

— UNFORGETTABLE GAMES:
FOR CELTIC AND TOMMY —

Dundee United 0 Celtic 1, Scottish Premier League, Tannadice, 22nd May 2008

Even if it was a sixth title for the club in eight years, there was never any prospect of a familiar air descending on the championship party on a balmy evening at Tannadice. Circumstances ensured that. However, the scale of the euphoria let loose after Gordon Strachan's side edged out Rangers still took the breath away. Former Celtic captain Tom Boyd, a veteran of four successful championship campaigns, watched from the stand with jaw dropping. "It was absolutely amazing – I've never seen a celebration like it," said a man who had been at the centre of what many considered to be unsurpassable scenes of joy when Celtic won the title to end Rangers' hopes of ten-in-a-row a decade earlier.

Emotions were raw because only two days earlier the Celtic players, and many fans who showered them with accolades and scarves at the end, had attended the funeral of their colleague, friend and personification of a Celtic man, Tommy Burns.

The players, in particular captain Stephen McManus, had heaped pressure on themselves by saying in the lead-up to the game that they were determined to claim the league crown in tribute to Burns. By doing precisely that there was palpable relief, amidst the post-match cavorting, that Burns's memory had been so fittingly honoured. At full-time, indeed, the squad and coaching staff donned T-shirts sporting Burns's picture above the words 'You'll always be with us' and dedicating the success to him.

Equally, the title meant so much to those on the pitch and in the stands because it had seemed highly unlikely just six weeks earlier when their rivals had a quadruple in their sights. Virtually all hope vanished when Celtic lost at home to Motherwell, to leave themselves six points behind the Ibrox men, who had two games in hand. A group of frothing supporters took this as the cue to urge Strachan to go. "Almost impossible" was how the manager publicly assessed his team's chances of retaining their title.

However, Celtic hauled themselves back into contention by winning six straight matches, back-to-back Old Firm victories chief among these. They did so as the Ibrox side, having to cram in games around their run to a UEFA Cup final they ultimately lost, dropped 12 crucial points.

It meant that when it came to the Thursday evening climax of a Premier League season extended because of Rangers' European commitments, Celtic knew a win would require their adversaries to beat Aberdeen by five goals at Pittodrie to snatch the championship on goal difference.

Any outcome could not be discounted after Celtic had lost the title in agonising circumstances on the final day in both 2003 and 2005. A painful hat-trick, though, became the longest of long shots when Aberdeen, whose antipathy for Rangers approaches that of Celtic, took the lead through Lee Miller after 63 minutes.

Then, in the 66th minute of an engrossing Tannadice encounter, Jan Vennegoor of Hesselink rose majestically to head in his 20th goal of the season from a Paul Hartley corner. When Darren Mackie bagged a second goal for the Pittodrie side in the 77th minute, the title celebrations down the road in Dundee began . . . and, such was the outpouring of emotion, they seemed to go on for weeks afterwards.

Dundee United: Zaluska, Dillon, Dods, Kenneth, Grainger, Flood, Kerr (Robb), Gomis, Swanson (Robertson), De Vries (Daly), Hunt
Celtic: Boruc, Hinkel, Caldwell, McManus, Naylor (Wilson), Nakamura (Scott Brown), Hartley, Robson, McGeady, McDonald, Vennegoor of Hesselink (Samaras)

— NAKA AND THE ART OF FREE-KICK INVENTION —

The Zen of Naka is the brilliant title of a biography on the life of Shunsuke Nakamura. Any discussion of the exciting Japanese playmaker tends to revolve around his divine dead-ball delivery, and with good reason. In his four years with Celtic after joining from Reggina in September 2005, he flighted, curled, looped, whipped, spun, arced, dipped and bent the ball to find the net 14 times with set-piece sorcery. His whole bag of tricks seemed to go into the awesome 32-yard effort against Manchester United in November 2006; a free kick given huge exposure around the world and instrumental to Celtic's first appearance in the Champions

League knock-out stages. While that was the most memorable of his dead-ball goals, the other 13 were pretty good too:

Date	Result
26th Oct 2005	Celtic 5 Motherwell 0
14th Jan 2006	Celtic 4 Kilmarnock 2
9th April 2006	Kilmarnock 1 Celtic 4
29th July 2006	Celtic 4 Kilmarnock 1
13th Sept 2006	Manchester Utd 3 Celtic 2
29th Oct 2006	Kilmarnock 1 Celtic 2
11th Nov 2006	Celtic 1 Manchester Utd 0
17th Feb 2007	Aberdeen 1 Celtic 2
22nd April 2007	Kilmarnock 1 Celtic 2
11th Aug 2007	Falkirk 1 Celtic 4
22nd Feb 2008	St Mirren 0 Celtic 1
31st Aug 2008	Celtic 2 Rangers 4
29th Oct 2008	Kilmarnock 1 Celtic 3
7th March 2009	Celtic 1 St Mirren 0

— CROSS-BORDER CONFRONTATIONS —

Celtic's results against English clubs in European competitions:

Date	Competition	Result
14th April 1966	Cup Winners' Cup	Celtic 1 Liverpool 0
19th April 1966	Cup Winners' Cup	Liverpool 2 Celtic 0
1st April 1970	European Cup	Leeds 0 Celtic 1
15th April 1970	European Cup	Celtic 2 Leeds 1
23rd Nov 1983	UEFA Cup	Nottingham Forest 0 Celtic 0
7th Dec 1983	UEFA Cup	Celtic 1 Nottingham Forest 2
16th Sept 1997	UEFA Cup	Celtic 2 Liverpool 2
30th Sept 1997	UEFA Cup	Liverpool 0 Celtic 0
31st Oct 2002	UEFA Cup	Celtic 1 Blackburn 0
14th Nov 2002	UEFA Cup	Blackburn 0 Celtic 2
13th Mar 2003	UEFA Cup	Celtic 1 Liverpool 1
20th Mar 2003	UEFA Cup	Liverpool 0 Celtic 2

13th Sept 2006	Champions Lge	Manchester United 3 Celtic 2
21st Nov 2006	Champions Lge	Celtic 1 Manchester United 0
21st Oct 2008	Champions Lge	Manchester United 3 Celtic 0
5th Nov 2008	Champions Lge	Celtic 1 Manchester United 1

— SCOTTISH CUP TRIUMPHS —

Celtic's record 34 wins in the Scottish Cup have come against the following opponents in the final:

Rangers, 7 times
Dundee United, 4 times
Hibernian, 4 times
Aberdeen, 3 times
Dunfermline, 3 times
Motherwell, 3 times
Airdrieonians, twice
Queens Park, twice
Clyde, once
Dundee, once
East Fife, once
Hamilton Academical, once
Hearts, once
St Mirren, once

— MISCELLANEOUS SEASONAL RECORDS —

Highest points total: 103 in 2001/02
Most league wins: 33 in 2001/02
Most home wins: 19 in 1921/22
Most away wins: 17 in 1915/16
Fewest defeats: 0 in 1897/98
Fewest home defeats: 0 on 21 occasions
Fewest away defeats: 0 on four occasions

Lowest points total: 21 in 1890/91
Fewest league wins: 8 in 1902/03
Fewest home wins: 4 in 1902/03
Fewest away wins: 3 on five occasions
Most defeats: 15 in 1947/48 and 1977/78
Most home defeats: 6 on five occasions
Most away defeats: 11 in 1977/78

Most goals scored: 116 in 1915/16
Most goals scored at home: 71 in 1935/36
Most goals scored away: 53 in 1967/68
Fewest goals conceded: 13 in 1897/98
Fewest goals conceded at home: 3 in 1910/11
Fewest goals conceded away: 6 in 1897/98

Fewest goals scored: 37 in 1989/90
Fewest goals scored at home: 16 in 1994/95
Fewest goals scored away: 14 in 1949/50
Most goals conceded: 59 in 1959/60
Most goals conceded at home: 31 in 1938/39
Most goals conceded away: 39 in 1964/65

Most draws: 20 in 1993/94
Most home draws: 11 in 1993/94
Most away draws: 11 in 1921/22
Fewest draws: 0 in 1895/96
Fewest home draws: 0 on five occasions
Fewest away draws: 0 on four occasions

— CELTIC'S COMPLETE LEAGUE RECORD —

SCOTTISH LEAGUE 1890/91 TO 1974/75

	Home						Away						
	P	W	D	L	F	A	W	D	L	F	A	Pts	Pos
1890/91	18	7	2	0	26	8	4	1	4	22	13	21	3rd
1891/92	22	10	1	0	32	6	6	2	3	30	15	35	2nd
1892/93	18	8	0	1	32	14	6	1	2	22	11	29	1st
1893/94	18	7	1	1	30	12	7	0	2	23	20	29	1st
1894/95	18	6	2	1	30	14	5	2	2	20	15	26	2nd
1895/96	18	8	0	1	39	9	7	0	2	25	16	30	1st
1896/97	18	6	2	1	20	5	4	2	3	22	13	24	4th
1897/98	18	8	1	0	30	7	7	2	0	26	6	33	1st
1898/99	18	7	0	2	28	13	4	2	3	23	20	24	3rd
1899/1900	18	6	2	1	25	14	3	5	1	21	13	25	2nd
1900/01	20	7	1	2	25	13	6	2	2	24	15	29	2nd
1901/02	18	5	2	2	19	15	6	2	1	19	13	26	2nd
1902/03	22	4	6	1	20	15	4	4	3	16	15	26	5th
1903/04	26	11	1	1	43	12	7	1	6	25	15	38	3rd
1904/05	26	8	4	1	31	15	10	1	2	37	16	41	1st
190506	30	13	0	2	36	8	11	1	3	40	11	49	1st
1906/07	34	13	4	0	40	14	10	5	2	40	16	55	1st
1907/08	34	15	2	0	57	11	9	5	3	29	16	55	1st
1908/09	34	11	3	3	36	10	12	2	3	35	14	51	1st
1909/10	34	13	4	0	38	9	11	2	4	25	13	54	1st
1910/11	34	11	4	2	31	3	4	7	6	17	15	41	5th
191112	34	14	3	0	38	11	3	8	6	20	22	45	2nd
1912/13	34	13	2	2	32	12	9	3	5	21	16	49	2nd
1913/14	38	15	3	1	45	6	15	2	2	36	8	65	1st
1914/15	38	18	1	0	56	10	12	4	3	35	15	65	1st
1915/16	38	15	3	1	64	13	17	0	2	52	10	67	1st
1916/17	38	13	5	1	38	8	14	5	0	41	9	64	1st
1917/18	34	11	4	2	34	13	13	3	1	32	13	55	2nd
1918/19	34	13	3	1	33	10	13	3	1	38	12	58	1st
1919/20	42	15	6	0	54	14	14	4	3	35	17	68	2nd
1920/21	42	16	3	2	50	15	14	3	4	36	20	66	2nd
1921/22	42	19	2	0	51	4	8	11	2	32	16	67	1st
1922/23	38	10	5	4	29	21	9	3	7	23	18	46	3rd

1923/24	38	11	5	3	36	15	6	7	6	20	18	46	3rd
1924/25	38	13	3	3	51	13	5	5	9	26	31	44	4th
1925/26	38	15	4	0	59	15	10	4	5	38	25	58	1st
1926/27	38	14	2	3	58	21	7	5	7	43	34	49	3rd
1927/28	38	14	3	2	56	13	9	6	4	37	26	55	2nd
1928/29	38	13	2	4	38	17	9	5	5	29	27	51	2nd
1929/30	38	12	1	6	52	21	10	4	5	36	25	49	4th
1930/31	38	16	2	1	64	14	8	8	3	37	20	58	2nd
1931/32	38	13	2	4	64	24	7	6	6	30	26	48	3rd
1932/33	38	13	3	3	47	18	7	5	7	28	26	48	4th
1933/34	38	12	5	2	47	20	6	6	7	31	33	47	3rd
1934/35	38	15	2	2	61	19	9	2	8	31	26	52	2nd
1935/36	38	17	1	1	71	16	15	1	3	44	17	66	1st
1936/37	38	14	3	2	59	26	8	5	6	30	32	52	3rd
1937/38	38	16	3	0	70	15	11	4	4	44	27	61	1st
1938/39	38	11	3	5	62	31	9	5	5	37	22	48	2nd
1939/40	5	2	0	1	4	3	1	0	1	3	4	6	*
1946/47	30	8	2	5	30	27	5	4	6	23	28	32	7th
1947/48	30	5	4	6	21	25	5	1	9	20	31	25	12th
1948/49	30	7	3	5	26	17	5	4	6	22	23	31	6th
1949/50	30	11	4	0	37	17	3	3	9	14	33	35	5th
1950/51	30	6	3	6	29	25	6	2	7	19	21	29	7th
1951/52	30	7	5	3	30	22	3	3	9	22	33	28	9th
1952/53	30	7	3	5	33	26	4	4	7	18	28	29	8th
1953/54	30	14	1	0	40	7	6	2	7	32	22	43	1st
1954/55	30	10	4	1	42	16	9	4	2	34	21	46	2nd
1955/56	34	9	4	4	31	18	7	5	5	24	21	41	5th
1956/57	34	9	6	2	33	14	6	2	9	25	29	38	5th
1957/58	34	7	6	4	42	22	12	2	3	42	25	46	3rd
1958/59	34	11	4	2	48	24	3	4	10	22	29	36	6th
1959/60	34	7	5	5	36	24	5	4	8	37	35	33	9th
1960/61	34	9	4	4	33	22	6	5	6	31	24	39	4th
1961/62	34	12	4	1	46	16	7	4	6	35	21	46	3rd
1962/63	34	10	3	4	33	16	9	3	5	43	28	44	4th
1963/64	34	13	3	1	61	16	6	6	5	28	18	47	3rd
1964/65	34	9	2	6	33	18	7	3	7	43	39	37	8th
1965/66	34	16	1	0	66	12	11	2	4	40	18	57	1st
1966/67	34	14	2	1	61	17	12	4	1	50	16	58	1st

	P	W	D	L	F	A	W	D	L	F	A	Pts	Pos
1967/68	34	14	3	0	53	14	16	0	1	53	10	63	1st
1968/69	34	12	3	2	50	19	11	5	1	39	13	54	1st
1969/70	34	12	2	3	54	18	15	1	1	42	15	57	1st
1970/71	34	15	1	1	43	7	11	5	2	46	16	56	1st
1971/72	34	15	1	1	48	14	13	3	1	48	14	60	1st
1972/73	34	14	3	0	47	10	12	2	3	46	18	57	1st
1973/74	34	12	4	1	51	12	11	3	3	31	15	53	1st
1974/75	32	11	2	4	47	20	9	3	5	34	21	45	3rd

*Season terminated due to onset of the Second World War.

PREMIER DIVISION 1975/76 TO 1996/97

	Home						Away						
	P	W	D	L	F	A	W	D	L	F	A	Pts	Pos
1975/76	36	10	5	3	35	18	11	1	6	36	24	48	2nd
1976/77	36	13	5	0	44	16	10	4	4	35	23	55	1st
1977/78	36	11	3	4	36	19	4	3	11	27	35	36	5th
1978/79	36	12	4	2	32	13	9	2	7	29	24	48	1st
1979/80	36	13	3	2	44	17	4	8	5	17	21	47	2nd
1980/81	36	12	3	3	47	18	14	1	3	37	19	56	1st
1981/82	36	12	5	1	41	16	12	2	4	38	17	55	1st
1982/83	36	12	3	3	44	18	13	2	3	46	18	55	2nd
1983/84	36	13	5	0	46	15	8	3	7	34	26	50	2nd
1984/85	36	12	3	3	43	12	10	5	3	34	18	52	2nd
1985/86	36	10	6	2	27	15	10	4	4	40	23	50	1st
1986/87	44	16	5	1	57	17	11	4	7	33	24	63	2nd
1987/88	44	16	5	1	42	11	15	5	2	37	12	72	1st
1988/89	36	13	1	4	35	18	8	3	7	31	26	46	3rd
1989/90	36	6	6	6	21	20	4	8	6	16	17	34	5th
1990/91	36	10	4	4	30	14	7	3	8	22	24	41	3rd
1991/92	44	15	3	4	47	20	11	7	4	41	22	62	3rd
1992/93	44	13	5	3	37	18	11	5	4	31	23	58	3rd
1993/94	44	8	11	3	26	21	7	9	6	25	17	50	4th
1994/95	36	6	8	4	16	14	5	10	3	23	19	51	4th
1995/96	36	12	5	1	40	12	12	6	0	34	13	83	2nd
1996/97	36	14	2	2	48	9	8	5	5	30	25	75	2nd

SCOTTISH PREMIER LEAGUE 1997/98 TO 2007/08

	Home						Away						
	P	W	D	L	F	A	W	D	L	F	A	Pts	Pos
1997/98	36	12	4	2	41	9	10	4	4	23	15	74	1st
1998/99	36	14	2	2	49	12	7	6	5	35	23	71	2nd
1999/2000	36	12	3	3	58	17	9	3	6	32	21	69	2nd
2000/01	38	17	1	1	48	11	13	3	2	42	18	97	1st
2001/02	38	18	1	0	51	9	15	3	1	43	9	103	1st
2002/03	38	18	1	0	56	12	13	3	3	42	14	97	2nd
2003/04	38	15	2	2	62	15	16	3	0	43	10	98	1st
2004/05	38	15	0	4	41	15	15	2	2	44	20	92	2nd
2005/06	38	14	4	1	41	15	14	3	2	52	22	91	1st
2006/07	38	16	1	2	36	13	10	5	4	29	21	84	1st
2007/08	38	14	4	1	42	7	14	1	4	42	19	89	1st
2008/09	38	14	4	1	48	13	10	6	3	32	20	82	2nd

Selected Bibliography:

A Celtic A – Z, Tom Campbell & Pat Woods (Greenfield Press, 1992)
An Alphabet of the Celts, Eugene McBride, Martin O'Connor & George Sheridan (ACL Colour Print & Polar Publishing, 1994)
Celtic: A Complete Record 1888-1992, Paul Lunney (Breedon Books, 1992)
Celtic: The Top 11 of Everything, Steve Morgan (Rough Guides, 2005)
The Essential History of Celtic, Graham McColl and George Sheridan (Headline, 1988)
The Glory and the Dream, Tom Campbell & Pat Woods (Grafton Books, 1987)
The Lisbon Lion: the book of Jock Stein, Alex Murphy (Toilet Books, 2007)
The Little Book of Celtic, Graham McColl (Carlton Books, 2004)
The Official Little Book of Celtic, Douglas Russell (Celtic, 2005)

Websites:

www.kerrydalestreet.com
www.keep-the-faith.net

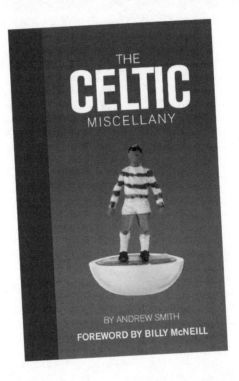

THE CELTIC MISCELLANY